Juicing for Beginners

Easy and Delicious Juicing Recipes for Weight Loss, Energy, Detox, Anti-aging, and So Much More

Dana Dittman

© Copyright 2022—All rights reserved.

The content contained within this book may not be reproduced, duplicated or transmitted without direct written permission from the author or the publisher.

Under no circumstances will any blame or legal responsibility be held against the publisher, or author, for any damages, reparation, or monetary loss due to the information contained within this book, either directly or indirectly.

Legal Notice:

This book is copyright protected. It is only for personal use. You cannot amend, distribute, sell, use, quote or paraphrase any part, or the content within this book, without the consent of the author or publisher.

Disclaimer Notice:

Please note the information contained within this document is for educational and entertainment purposes only. All effort has been executed to present accurate, up to date, reliable, complete information. No warranties of any kind are declared or implied. Readers acknowledge that the author is not engaged in the rendering of legal, financial, medical or professional advice. The content within this book has been derived from various sources. Please consult a licensed professional before attempting any techniques outlined in this book.

By reading this document, the reader agrees that under no circumstances is the author responsible for any losses, direct or indirect, that are incurred as a result of the use of the information contained within this document, including, but not limited to, errors, omissions, or inaccuracies.

Table of Contents

INTRODUCTION 1

CHAPTER 1: JUICES FOR EYESIGHT 7

    BRIGHT EYES JUICE 8
    CELERY, CARROT AND SPINACH JUICE 9
    SPINACH, KALE & BROCCOLI JUICE 9
    CARROT TREAT 10
    ORANGE AND GINGER JUICE 11
    CUCUMBER WITH CELERY AND CARROTS JUICE 12
    TROPICAL CARROT APPLE JUICE... 13
    CARROT AND CILANTRO JUICE 14
    THE VEGGIE DELIGHT 14
    SUNSET SURPRISE.. 15
    LEEK AND BROCCOLI JUICE 16

CHAPTER 2: JUICES FOR HEALTHY HEART 19

    BEET AND DATE JUICE 19
    HEALTHY TOMATO JUICE 20
    CURRY IN A HURRY 21
    TOMATO AND BEETROOT JUICE... 22
    THE BIG RED JUICE 23
    SWEET AND SOUR TOMATO BASIL JUICE 24
    TOMATO, BEET, AND LEMON JUICE 24
    PEACH, ORANGE AND TOMATO GREEN JUICE 25
    THE CHOLESTEROL FIGHTER JUICE 26
    RED CABBAGE JUICE 27

CHAPTER 3: JUICES FOR KIDNEYS 29

    KIDNEY CLEANSE JUICE 30
    CUCUMBER, CELERY, AND CARROT JUICE 31
    THE GREEN DIURETIC.. 32

- WATERCRESS AND CARROT JUICE 33
- CILANTRO DETOX JUICE 34
- HERBS AND CUCUMBER GREEN JUICE.. 35

CHAPTER 4: JUICES FOR HEALTHY SKIN 37

- SKIN TONIC JUICE... 37
- MIRACLE JUICE FOR GLOWING SKIN 38
- SPINACH JUICE... 39
- GLOWING SKIN GREEN JUICE... 40
- GLOWING SKIN CELERY JUICE 41
- DEEP RED JUICE 42
- CARROT AND GINGER JUICE 42
- PINEAPPLE AND CUCUMBER JUICE 43
- PAPAYA JUICE... 44
- BROCCOLI JUICE 45
- KALE AND ALOE VERA JUICE 45

CHAPTER 5: JUICES FOR IMPROVED BRAIN FUNCTIONING... 47

- BRAIN BOOSTING JUICE 48
- BRAIN BOOSTER JUICE 49
- PAPAYA AND GUAVA JUICE 50
- THE PEPPER MAGIC DRINK 51
- BERRY AND APPLE JUICE 52
- MIXED BERRY JUICE... 53

CHAPTER 5: JUICES FOR HAPPY STATE OF MIND 55

- ORANGE AND MANGO JUICE 56
- STRAWBERRY, CARROT, AND MANGO JUICE 57
- BANANA AND MANGO JUICE 58
- PINEAPPLE AND AVOCADO JUICE 59
- AVOCADO AND TOMATO JUICE 60

CHAPTER 6: JUICES TO SLOW DOWN AGING 61

- RED CABBAGE JUICE 61
- ANTI-AGING CITRUS JUICE TO REDUCE WRINKLES........................... 62
- PINK JUICE FOR ANTI-AGING.. 63
- APPLE AND BLUEBERRY JUICE 64
- POMEGRANATE AND MINT JUICE 65

Anti-aging Green Monster Juice 66

CHAPTER 7: JUICES FOR BONE HEALTH 69

Ease Your Joints Juice 70
Grapefruit Juice 71
All Green Juice 72
Anti-inflammatory Tonic 73
Spinach and Kale Green Juice 74
Anti-inflammatory Citrus Juice 75
Tomato and Celery Juice 76
Juice to Prevent Osteoporosis 77

CHAPTER 8: ANTIOXIDANT JUICES 79

Cranberry Cucumber Juice 79
Cranberry Apple Juice 80
Strawberry Watermelon Juice 81
Kiwi Juice 82

CHAPTER 9: COLON CLEANSING JUICES 83

Cleansing Green Juice 84
Beetroot Juice 85
Prune Juice for Constipation Relief 86
Pineapple and Kiwi Juice 87
Morning Juice 87
Beet Juice to Relieve Constipation 89
Apple and Kiwi Punch 90
Green Orange Bowel Booster 91

CHAPTER 10: DETOX JUICES 93

Green Detox Juice 93
The Newbie 94
The Detoxer 95
Green Beet Juice 96
Green Cucumber Juice 97

CHAPTER 11: JUICES FOR THE DIGESTIVE SYSTEM 99

Digestion-soothing Juice 100
Gut Healing Juice 101

- Juice for Constipation Relief 102
- Juice for Upset Stomach 102
- Carrot Apple Juice for Diarrhea... 103
- Cucumber Juice for Indigestion and Constipation Relief 104

CHAPTER 12: JUICES FOR ANEMIA.......................................107

- Parsley Juice 107
- Beet, Orange, and Carrot Juice.. 108
- High Iron Vegetable Juice... 109
- Iron Boost... 110
- Blueberry and Spinach Juice 111
- Iron Boosting Sweet and Tart Green Juice 112
- Leafy Greens 113

CHAPTER 13: JUICES FOR LOWERING BLOOD PRESSURE 115

- Green Juice 116
- Pineapple and Celery Juice 117
- Beet, Carrot, Pineapple, and Orange Juice............................ 118
- Pear and Zucchini Juice 119
- Beet, Carrot, Pineapple, and Orange Juice............................ 120
- Tropical Carrot Juice.. 121

CHAPTER 14: ANTI-INFLAMMATORY JUICES 123

- Green Pineapple Juice 124
- Carrot, Pineapple, and Turmeric Juice.................................. 125
- Orange Tonic 126
- Cinnamon Spiced Tropical Juice.. 127
- Grape and Kale Juice 128
- Apple and Fennel Juice 129
- Blueberry and Apple Juice 130
- Watermelon Juice 131

CHAPTER 15: ANTIOXIDANT JUICES.....................................133

- Cranberry and Pomegranate Juice 134
- Cranberry and Cucumber Juice... 135
- Antioxidant Power-up Juice 136
- Red Lettuce Juice 137
- Sweet Potato and Cabbage Juice 138

CHAPTER 16: ANTI-CANCER JUICES AND JUICES FOR CANCER PATIENTS 139

- Orange and Cranberry Juice 140
- Orange, Carrot, and Apple Juice 141
- Breakfast Blend 142
- Blueberry Blast 142
- Orange Sunset 143
- Pink Power 144
- Orange Blast 145
- Cranberry Apple Juice 146
- Ginger Cinnamon Carrot Butternut Squash Juice 147
- Carrot Juice 148
- Green Machine 149
- Banana, Apple and Ginger Juice 150
- Protein Power Juice 151
- Tart Green Juice 152

CHAPTER 17: JUICES FOR DIABETICS 153

- Bitter Melon Juice 154
- Apple and Cucumber Juice 155
- Strawberry and Kale Juice 155
- Cucumber, Pear, Ginger, and Lemon 156
- Apple and Carrot Juice 157
- Cabbage and Apple Juice 158
- Mixed Vegetable Juice 159

CHAPTER 18: JUICES FOR PREGNANCY 161

- Green Juice 161
- Green Orange Juice 162
- Juice to Relieve Morning Sickness 163
- Veggie and Fruit Juice 164
- Hydrating Blended Juice 165
- Green Juice for Nausea 166

CHAPTER 19: JUICES FOR HEALTHY HAIR 167

- Potato Juice 167
- Fresh Orange Juice 168

- Amla Juice 169
- Carrot Juice 170
- Aloe Vera Juice 171
- Spinach Juice 172

CHAPTER 20: JUICES FOR HEALTHY LIVER 173

- Liver Detoxifier 173
- The Liver Scrubber Juice 174
- Herbs and Asparagus Juice 175

CHAPTER 21: THIRTY DAYS OF JUICING 177

- Day 1: Ginger and lemon Juice 177
- Day 2: Mint and Berries Juice 178
- Day 3: Sweet Pineapple Juice 178
- Day 4: Spritzy Pomegranate-Blueberry Juice 179
- Day 5: Savory Carrot Juice 180
- Day 6: Lavender and Pineapple Juice 180
- Day 7: Cucumber and Apple Juice 181
- Day 8: Bundling Carrots, Apples and Beets Juice 181
- Day 9: Smooth Juice of Apple Beet and Carrot 182
- Day 10: Tropical Paradise 183
- Day 11: Apples, Cantaloupe, and Honeydew Juice 183
- Day 12: Cucumber and Apple Juice 184
- Day 13: Sleek Beet Celeriac Carrot Juice 185
- Day 14: Carrot and Tomato Juice 185
- Day 15: Carrots, Pineapples and Oranges Juice 186
- Day 16: Citrus cascade Juice 187
- Day 17: Beets and Oranges 187
- Day 18: Pear and Fennel Juice 188
- Day 19: Tomatoes and Cucumber Juice 188
- Day 20: Ginger and Blackberries Juice 189
- Day 21: Apples and Carrot Juice 189
- Day 22: The Green Delicacy Juice 190
- Day 23: Spinach and Lemon Juice 191
- Day 24: Yellowish Gold Juice 191
- Day 25: Celery and Spinach Juice 192
- Day 26: Oranges and Cranberry Juice 192
- Day 27: Kale and Ginger Juice 193

        Day 28: Lime and Apple Juice 194
        Day 29: Sour and Smooth Lemon Juice 194
        Day 30: Minty Strawberries and Pineapple Juice 195

CONCLUSION 197

REFERENCES 199

Introduction

Do you want to lose weight without following any worrisome crash diets? Do you want to consume well-balanced and nutritional meals but don't have the time to cook? Are you usually in a rush and are looking for ideas to eat healthy? Well, what if you can get all the nutrition needed within a couple of minutes? Yes, you read it right! You can do this by juicing!

Through juicing you can extract the nutrition from vegetables and fruit. When you juice, the ingredients, the pulp and seeds are removed from them. The product you have in the end will contain a large quantity of minerals, antioxidants and vitamins.

You can either squeeze the vegetables and fruit by using a juicer or can use a blender. It is best to choose from either a centrifugal or cold-press juicer. The former grinds the vegetable and fruit into pulp using a cutting blade. The blade moves at a very high speed and the spin separates the solids and juices. The latter crushes the fruit and vegetable and presses them slowly to remove as much of the juice from the ingredients. While the process of extracting juices is different, the nutritional quality is the same.

Why do you think people drink juices? Since these juices have most of the nutrients a person needs, they can be used as a supplement for meals. If you are on a diet and want to limit your consumption of unhealthy food, you can choose to substitute your meals with juices. You can increase your nutrient intake which you normally would not consume otherwise. Some people also use juicing for detoxification and cleansing. You can eliminate the consumption of solid food and drink only juice at least three times a week. This will cleanse your body and get rid of toxins.

Most people unfortunately do not consume enough nutrients through their diet. It is also unfortunate that most foods consumed now do not have the required nutrient level in them. This is due to the methods used to transport the produce from the source to the supermarket or the processing methods used. Now, people are under constant stress and stay in polluted environments. This also increases your body's need for some nutrients.

Vegetables and fruit are rich in antioxidants, plant compounds, minerals and vitamins. These protect you from different diseases and keep your body healthy. If you cannot consume the required quantity of vegetables and fruit in your diet, the best way to consume the required quantity is through juicing. People's nutrient levels of Vitamin C, selenium, Vitamin E, folate and beta carotene improved when they consumed mixed vegetable and fruit juices (Kiefer I et al., 2004). People's antioxidant, folate, Vitamin E, Vitamin C and beta carotene levels improved when they drank blended powder concentrate juices, and fresh vegetable and fruit juices (Esfahani A et al., 2011).

Do juices protect you from diseases?

Research shows that whole vegetables and fruit increase your body's immunity and reduce the risk of numerous diseases. The benefits of vegetables and fruit are due to the fiber and antioxidant content present in them. Since antioxidants are bound to fiber, you would need to consume enough of it for it to release into your digestive system.

A significant intake of vegetables and fruit can improve your health in many ways. Fresh vegetable and fruit juices can reduce the risk of heart disease, cholesterol levels and blood pressure. Further, these juices can also reduce the markers of oxidative stress and homocysteine, thereby improving your heart health.

Is it important to include fiber?

As mentioned earlier, when you prepare juices, you get rid of the pulp which contains a lot of the fiber. Let us look at some of the benefits of fiber:

- An increase in fiber lowers type 2 diabetes, risk of heart diseases and obesity.

- When you increase soluble fiber in your diet, you can improve cholesterol and blood sugar levels.

Drinking apple juice reduced the levels of bad or LDL cholesterol by 6.9% (Ravn-Haren G et al., 2013). According to the team, this effect is due to the fiber found in the apples. Research also shows that people feel full when they consume the required fiber from fruit and vegetables.

This brings us to the question– "Should I add fiber to my juice?". You definitely should add fiber to the juice. The quantity of sugar you must add is dependent on the type of appliance you use. You can include the fiber from the juicer into the juice or even add it to other foods. It is better to do this instead of throwing the pulp away.

Some juicing tips before you get started:

- Wash all ingredients before using, you don't need to dry or wipe them.

- While juicing, always start with the most delicate ingredients, such as herbs and leafy greens.

- Then move on with the soft veggies and fruit such as berries, tomatoes, etc.

- Top off with hard veggies and fruit such as celery, apples, etc.

- Drink your juice fresh when you make it.

- Juices can be consumed at any time of the day and as a substitute for any meal.

- To make your juicing journey a success, make sure you have at least one nutritious meal everyday.

Now that you have a fair idea about juicing, dive into the book to find out what you can do with different fruit and vegetables. Over the course of this book, you will come across different recipes you can use to prepare juices and choose the best type of juice for you depending on the issue you want to deal with. You will come across different recipes to treat your skin, cleanse your system, reduce the risk of heart diseases, reduce the risk of cancer and much more.

Thank you for purchasing the book. I hope you get all the information you are looking for.

Chapter 1:

Juices for Eyesight

In this chapter, you will find recipes to improve your eyesight. The vegetables and fruit in the recipes are rich in vitamin A and other nutrients needed to improve your eyesight. Some of the recipes contain carrots, and this vegetable has large quantities of beta-carotene. Your body converts this compound into vitamin A, and this vitamin can improve your eye health. Beets contain zeaxanthin and lutein, and these compounds support both retinal and macular health. Other ingredients used in the recipes are rich in bioflavonoids, and these improve your vision and eye health.

Berries also contain different antioxidants, and these help to reduce oxidative stress. It is important for you to consume foods rich in antioxidants to improve your eyesight. As you grow older, different parts of your eye will begin to degenerate, but the antioxidants and other nutrients in berries can slow down the process of aging. These ingredients can also preserve your eye health. It is best to have as many natural colors on your plate as possible.

Bright Eyes Juice

Serves: 1

Ingredients:

- 2 cups parsley
- 2 cups rocket & lettuce leaves
- 2 carrots
- 2 cups spinach
- 4 large kale leaves

Directions:

1. Wash all the vegetables and chop into chunks.
2. Place parsley, lettuce, carrots, spinach, and kale in a juicer and extract the juice.
3. Alternately, blend together all ingredients in a blender with a little water until smooth. Strain the juice.
4. Pour into a glass and serve.

Celery, Carrot and Spinach Juice

Serves: 2

Ingredients:

- 8 medium carrots, peeled, chopped
- 2 bunches spinach, chopped
- 6 stalks celery, chopped

Directions:

1. Wash the vegetables and chop into chunks. Juice together all the ingredients in a juicer.
2. Pour into glasses. Serve with crushed ice.

Spinach, Kale & Broccoli Juice

Serves: 1

Ingredients:

- 1 teaspoon chia seeds
- 1 cup kale
- 1 cup spinach
- 1 ½ cups water

- 2 green apples
- 10 broccoli florets

Directions:

1. Steam the broccoli for 2 minutes.
2. While the broccoli is steaming, wash the greens and apples and chop into chunks.
3. In a blender, add broccoli, apples, greens, chia seeds, and water and blend until smooth.
4. Strain the juice in a tall glass and serve.

Carrot Treat

Serves: 2

Ingredients:

- 2 oranges
- 4 beets
- 2 cups spinach
- ¼ red cabbage
- 6 carrots
- Juice of a lemon
- 1 cup fresh pineapple chunks

Directions:

1. Wash all the vegetables and fruits. Chop the vegetables into chunks.
2. Peel the oranges and separate the segments.
3. Add all the fruits and vegetables into a juicer and extract the juice.
4. Pour into 2 glasses.

Orange and Ginger Juice

Serves: 2

Ingredients:

- 6–7 carrots
- 2 inches fresh ginger
- 4 oranges

Directions:

1. Wash the oranges, carrots, and ginger. Chop carrots into chunks.
2. Peel the oranges and separate the segments.
3. Place the oranges, carrots, and ginger in the juicer and extract the juice.
4. Pour into tall glasses and serve.

Cucumber With Celery and Carrots Juice

Serves: 2

Ingredients:

- 2 bunches parsley
- 4 sticks celery, chopped
- 1 cucumber, chopped
- 6 medium carrots, chopped

Directions:

1. Wash the vegetables and chop into bite size pieces.
2. Juice together all the vegetables in a juicer.
3. Pour into glasses. Serve with crushed ice.

Tropical Carrot Apple Juice

Serves: 2

Ingredients:

- 1 cup chopped papaya
- 8 medium carrots
- 2 large apples, cored
- 2 cups fresh pineapple chunks
- 2 inches fresh ginger
- 1 kiwi fruit

Directions:

1. Wash ginger, carrots, apples, and kiwi and chop into chunks.
2. Juice together the carrots, apples, kiwi, pineapple, papaya, and ginger in a juicer.
3. Strain the juice.
4. Pour into glasses. Add some ice cubes if desired and serve.

Carrot and Cilantro Juice

Serves: 1

Ingredients:

- 4 carrots, chopped into chunks
- Juice of a lemon
- 2 cups chopped cilantro
- Himalayan black salt to taste (optional)

Directions:

1. Juice the carrots and cilantro in the juicer.
2. Pour into a glass. Add lemon juice and salt and stir.
3. Serve with crushed ice.

The Veggie Delight

Serves: 2

Ingredients:

- 4 carrots, chopped
- 4 oranges

- 2 stalks celery
- 3 large stems of broccoli
- ½ head lettuce
- ½ small cabbage green or red, cut into pieces

Directions

1. Wash the vegetables and chop into chunks. Peel the oranges and separate them into segments.
2. Juice together all the vegetables and oranges in a juicer.
3. Pour into glasses. Serve with ice cubes.

Sunset Surprise

Serves: 2

Ingredients:

- 2 medium yellow tomatoes
- 2 apples, cored
- 2 oranges
- 8 large carrots

Directions:

1. Wash the vegetables and fruits.

2. Cut the tomatoes and apples into wedges. Peel the oranges and separate the segments.
3. Place the tomatoes in the juicer followed by orange, apples, and the carrots and extract the juice.
4. Pour the juice into tall glasses and serve right away.

Leek and Broccoli Juice

Serves: 2

Ingredients:

- 1 cup chopped leek
- Pepper to taste
- 1 tablespoon lime juice
- 2 cups broccoli florets
- 2 cups baby spinach
- Salt to taste
- ½ cup water

Directions:

1. Wash all the vegetables. Add leeks, broccoli, spinach, and water into a blender. Blend them all until smooth.

2. Strain the juice. Add more water if the juice is thick and stir.
3. Add salt, pepper and lime juice and stir.
4. Pour into glasses, add crushed ice and serve.

Chapter 2:

Juices for Healthy Heart

There are certain fruits and vegetables that are packed with nutrients that can give your heart and other parts of the cardiovascular system a scientifically significant boost. This chapter contains juicing recipes for a healthy heart.

The fruit and vegetables used in these recipes improve your hemoglobin levels, reduce cholesterol levels and lowers blood sugar. These ingredients are rich in carotenoids, and these act as antioxidants in your body. They also have enough vitamins, minerals and fiber which improve your cardiovascular health. Some of these juices can help to improve your blood flow thereby reducing the formation of blood clots.

Beet and Date Juice

Serves: 2

Ingredients:

- 2 beets

- 1 inch fresh ginger
- 3 cups water
- 4 medjool dates, pitted
- 4 tablespoons pumpkin seeds

Directions:

1. Wash the vegetables.
2. Peel the beets and ginger and chop into chunks. Pit the dates and chop into pieces.
3. Add beets, dates, ginger, water, and pumpkin seeds into a blender and blend until very smooth. Strain the juice.
4. Pour into 2 glasses and serve with ice.

Healthy Tomato Juice

Serves: 2

Ingredients:

- 10 ounces tomatoes
- Sweetener to taste
- 1 tablespoon lemon juice

Directions:

1. Wash the tomatoes and cut into quarters.
2. Place tomatoes in the juicer and extract the juice.
3. Add sweetener and lemon juice and stir.
4. Pour into glasses and serve with ice.

Curry in a Hurry

Serves: 2

Ingredients:

- 5 large tomatoes
- 2 bunches spinach
- 2 beets
- 1 teaspoon curry powder
- A pinch of salt or to taste

Directions:

1. Wash all the vegetables and chop into chunks.
2. Add tomatoes, spinach, and beets into the juicer. Extract the juice.
3. Add curry powder and salt and stir.
4. Pour into glasses and serve with ice.

Tomato and Beetroot Juice

Serves: 2

Ingredients:

- 5 beets
- 6 tablespoons lime juice
- 5 tomatoes
- 1 cup mint leaves

Directions:

1. Wash the vegetables. Chop the beets and tomatoes into wedges.
2. Add beets, tomatoes, lime juice, and mint leaves into a blender and blend until smooth. Strain the juice.
3. Pour into glasses and serve.

The Big Red Juice

Serves: 2

Ingredients:

- 2 red apples, cored
- 2 large tomatoes
- 2 carrots
- 2 beets

Directions:

1. Wash the apples and vegetables and chop into chunks.
2. Place apples, tomatoes, and carrots in a juicer and extract the juice.
3. You can also add the ingredients into a blender and blend until smooth. Strain the juice and pour into glasses. If you find it too thick, dilute it with water.
4. Serve with ice cubes.

Sweet and Sour Tomato Basil Juice

Serves: 2

Ingredients:

- 6 vine tomatoes, chopped
- 1 cup basil
- 2 bunches grapes

Directions:

1. Wash the tomatoes, basil, and grapes. Chop tomatoes into thick wedges.
2. Place basil, tomatoes, and grapes in a juicer and extract the juice.
3. Pour into glasses and serve with ice.

Tomato, Beet, and Lemon Juice

Serves: 2

Ingredients:

- 8 Roma tomatoes
- 2 cucumbers

- 4 beets
- Juice of a lemon

Directions:

1. Wash the vegetables and chop into chunks.
2. Juice together tomatoes, cucumber and beets in a juicer.
3. Pour into glasses. Add lemon juice and stir.
4. Serve with ice.

Peach, Orange and Tomato Green Juice

Serves: 2

Ingredients:

- 4 kale leaves
- 1 peach, pitted
- 4 oranges
- 1 large tomato
- 1 lemon peeled, halved
- 2 teaspoons ground pumpkin seeds

Directions:

1. Wash the oranges and vegetables. Peel the orange and separate the segments. Chop tomatoes and peach into wedges.
2. Juice together oranges, peach, tomato, kale and lemon in a juicer.
3. Pour into glasses. Add a teaspoon of ground pumpkin seeds in each glass.
4. Stir well.
5. Serve with crushed ice.

The Cholesterol Fighter Juice

Serves: 2

Ingredients:

- 2 medium size heads Romaine lettuce
- 6 Swiss chard leaves
- 2 inch piece ginger
- 2 cucumbers
- 2 medium size Fuji apples, cored
- 2 navel oranges, (optional)

Directions:

1. Wash the vegetables and fruits.
2. Stack the Swiss chard leaves together and roll them up. It becomes easier to juice. Do the same with lettuce as well.
3. Chop apples and cucumbers into chunks.
4. Juice together the apples, cucumbers, Swiss chard, ginger, Romaine lettuce, and oranges if using.
5. Pour into glasses. Serve with crushed ice.

Red Cabbage Juice

Serves: 2

Ingredients:

- 4 oranges
- 4 sticks celery
- 2 inches fresh turmeric
- 3 large beets
- ½ small red cabbage

Directions:

1. Wash the vegetables and oranges.

2. Peel the oranges and separate them into segments.
3. Chop the beets and celery into bite size pieces. Shred the cabbage.
4. Place oranges, celery, turmeric, beets, and cabbage in a juicer and extract the juice.
5. You can also place all the ingredients in a blender with a little water and blend until smooth. Strain the juice.
6. Pour into glasses and serve with ice.

Chapter 3:

Juices for Kidneys

Since your kidneys work on regulating the fluid levels in your body, it is important for you to consume the required quantities of fluid to enable them to work to the best of their abilities.

Your kidneys hold a lot of toxins since most of the toxins move through your body and are removed from your system through your urine. You can use juicing to remove any toxins in your body, thereby reducing the volume of toxins stored in your body. Some of the recipes in this chapter include cruciferous vegetables, and these improve your liver and kidneys. They contain phytochemicals which improve detoxification enzyme levels thereby preventing damage. These juices also reduce the risk of inflammation.

Kidney Cleanse Juice

Serves: 2

Ingredients:

- 2 apples, cored
- 4 medium carrots
- 8 medium cucumbers
- 2 medium beets
- 4 sticks celery
- 2 oranges

Directions:

1. Wash all the fruits and vegetables.
2. Chop the apples, beets, cucumbers, and carrots into chunks.
3. Cut celery into 2 inch pieces.
4. Peel the oranges and separate the segments.
5. Place apples, carrots, cucumbers, beets, celery, and oranges in a juicer and extract the juice.
6. You can also place all the ingredients in a blender and blend until smooth.
7. Strain the juice if you are blending the ingredients.
8. Pour juice into glasses and serve with ice.

Cucumber, Celery, and Carrot Juice

Serves: 2

Ingredients:

- 2 bunches parsley
- 4 sticks celery
- 1 large cucumber
- 6 medium carrots

Directions:

1. Wash the vegetables.
2. Chop cucumbers and carrots into chunks.
3. Chop the greens and celery as well.
4. Juice together parsley, celery, cucumber, and carrots in a juicer.
5. Pour the juice into glasses. Serve with crushed ice.

The Green Diuretic

Serves: 2

Ingredients:

- 2 medium cucumbers
- 2 small carrots
- 4 cups spinach
- 6 stalks celery with leaves
- 2 green apples

Directions:

1. Wash the vegetables and apples. Chop them into chunks.
2. Juice together the ingredients alternating green apple and cucumber with greens and lastly the carrots.
3. Pour into glasses. Serve with crushed ice.

Watercress and Carrot Juice

Serves: 2

Ingredients:

- 4-5 large carrots
- 1 cup watercress
- Salt to taste
- Freshly ground pepper to taste

Directions:

1. Wash carrots and watercress. Chop carrots into chunks.
2. Add watercress and carrots into the juicer and extract the juice.
3. Pour into glasses. Stir in salt and pepper to taste. Serve with ice if desired.

Cilantro Detox Juice

Serves: 2

Ingredients:

- 2 bunches fresh cilantro
- 2 limes
- 2 lemons
- 6 small cucumbers
- 3 inches fresh ginger

Directions:

1. Wash the vegetables. Peel lemons and limes and cut into 2 halves.
2. Chop cucumbers into chunks. Chop cilantro into pieces.
3. Place cilantro in the juicer and extract the juice. Next add ginger followed by limes and lemons.
4. Lastly add cucumbers.
5. Pour juice into glasses and serve.

Herbs and Cucumber Green Juice

Serves: 2

Ingredients:

- ½ - 1 bunch parsley
- ½ large bunch celery
- 1 bunch basil
- 2 cucumbers
- 1 inch fresh ginger
- 1 lime or lemon
- 2 inches fresh turmeric (optional)

Directions:

1. Wash the greens, cucumbers, and ginger.
2. Chop cucumbers into chunks. Peel ginger and turmeric and cut into slices.
3. Chop the greens as well. Peel the lemon and cut into halves or quarters.
4. Juice together parsley, celery, basil, cucumber, lemon, turmeric, and ginger in a juicer.
5. Pour juice into glasses. Serve with crushed ice.

Chapter 4:

Juices for Healthy Skin

We are exposed to different pollutants in the environment, and these toxins affect our skin. Not many of us are aware of how to get rid of these toxins, and we use a million different products to improve our skin. Instead of using different chemicals on your skin, you can drink the juices mentioned in this chapter to cleanse any toxins in your skin and get rid of blemishes.

Skin Tonic Juice

Serves: 2

Ingredients:

- 4 cucumbers
- 2 cups chopped kale
- 2 mangoes, peeled
- 2 cups chopped spinach
- 1 cup cilantro
- Juice of a lemon (optional)
- Coconut water ice cubes, as required

Directions:

1. Pour some coconut water into ice cube trays. Freeze until set. Use as many as required.
2. Chop mango and cucumber into chunks.
3. Add cucumber, kale, mangoes, spinach and cilantro to a blender. Blend until smooth. Add a little water and blend until smooth. Strain the juice.
4. Pour juice into glasses. Add coconut water ice cubes. Let the flavors blend for a few minutes.
5. Stir and serve.

Miracle Juice for Glowing Skin

Serves: 2

Ingredients:

- 1 apple, cored
- 1 cup pineapple chunks
- 1 cucumber
- 2 cups water

Directions:

1. Wash the apple and cucumber.

2. Chop the apples and cucumber into chunks.
3. Add apple, cucumber, pineapple, and water into a blender. Blend the ingredients until smooth. Strain the juice.
4. Pour into 2 glasses. Serve with ice if desired.

Spinach Juice

Serves: 2

Ingredients:

- 2 cups chopped spinach
- 2 inches fresh ginger
- 2 cups water
- 1 cucumber
- 4 tablespoons fresh lemon juice

Directions:

1. Wash the vegetables.
2. Peel the cucumber and chop into chunks. Peel the ginger and cut into slices.
3. Place spinach, ginger, water, and cucumber in a blender and blend until smooth.
4. Strain the juice.
5. Pour into glasses. Add ice and serve.

Glowing Skin Green Juice

Serves: 1

Ingredients:

- 2 large apples, cored
- 4 kale leaves
- 3 celery sticks

Directions:

1. Wash the apples and vegetables.
2. Chop into chunks.
3. Cut the celery into about 2-inch pieces.
4. Stack the kale leaves and roll them up.
5. Place the apples, celery, and kale in the juicer and extract the juice. You can also blend together all the ingredients in a blender until smooth. Strain the juice if you are blending them in a blender.
6. Pour into a glass and serve.

Glowing Skin Celery Juice

Serves: 1

Ingredients:

- 1 cup celery leaves
- 1 teaspoon lemon juice
- ½ cup water
- ½ medium cucumber
- 1 heaped tablespoon Dulse seaweed flakes

Directions:

1. Wash the vegetables and chop into chunks.
2. Place celery, lemon juice, water, cucumber, and Dulse seaweed flakes in a blender and blend until smooth. Strain the juice if desired.
3. Pour into a glass and serve.

Deep Red Juice

Serves: 2

Ingredients:

- 2 beets
- 6 stalks celery
- 1 green apple, cored
- ½ cup pomegranate seeds

Directions:

1. Wash the vegetables and apple.
2. Chop beets, celery, and apple into chunks.
3. Add beets, apple, celery, and pomegranate seeds into a juicer and extract the juice.
4. Serve with ice.

Carrot and Ginger Juice

Serves: 2

Ingredients:

- 6 carrots

- Juice of a lemon
- 2 inches fresh ginger
- Honey to taste (optional)

Directions:

1. Wash the carrots and ginger.
2. Peel and chop ginger and carrots into small pieces.
3. Add carrots, ginger and some water into a blender and blend until very smooth.
4. Strain the juice. Stir in lemon juice and honey if using.
5. Serve with ice.

Pineapple and Cucumber Juice

Serves: 2

Ingredients:

- 2 cups pineapple chunks
- 2 cucumbers
- A handful fresh mint leaves
- A handful fresh spinach (optional)

Directions:

1. Wash cucumbers, spinach, and mint leaves.
2. Peel and chop cucumbers into chunks.
3. Add pineapple, cucumbers, spinach, and mint leaves into a blender and blend until smooth. Strain the juice if desired.
4. Pour into glasses and serve garnished with some torn mint leaves.

Papaya Juice

Serves: 2

Ingredients:

- 1 ½ cups papaya
- 1 tablespoon flaxseeds
- Honey to taste (optional)

Directions:

1. Blend together papaya, flaxseeds, and some water in a blender until smooth.
2. Pour into glasses. Add honey to taste if desired.
3. Stir and serve.

Broccoli Juice

Serves: 1

Ingredients:

- ½ head broccoli
- 1 tablespoon flaxseeds

Directions:

1. Wash broccoli and chop into florets.
2. Add flaxseeds, broccoli and some water into a blender and blend until very smooth.
3. Serve with ice.

Kale and Aloe Vera Juice

Serves: 1

Ingredients:

- 1 cup fresh aloe vera gel
- A handful kale leaves
- A handful parsley

Directions:

1. Cut a piece of fresh aloe vera leaf. Peel and remove the gel.
2. Wash kale and parsley. Remove hard ribs from the kale leaves.
3. Add kale, parsley, and aloe vera gel into a blender and blend until smooth.
4. Serve with ice.

Chapter 5:

Juices for Improved Brain Functioning

The brain is the control center of your body and is in charge of all conscious and unconscious decisions you make. Whether it is breathing and maintaining body temperature or a conscious decision to move, the brain does it all. Consuming healthy and wholesome fruits and vegetables is the best way to ensure this energy-hungry organ functions effectively and efficiently. Research shows that carrots, tomatoes, ginger, cucumber and other ingredients have antioxidants which can improve brain functions and reduce the risk of developing Alzheimer's and other diseases.

Brain Boosting Juice

Serves: 2

Ingredients:

- 3–4 beetroots with greens
- 4 carrots
- 1 ½ cucumbers
- ½ cup water

Directions:

1. Wash the vegetables well. Chop the beets, beet greens, cucumbers, and carrots into chunks and put them into a blender.
2. Add water and blend until smooth.
3. Strain the juice.
4. Pour into glasses and serve with ice.

Brain Booster Juice

Serves: 2

Ingredients:

- 2 large sweet potatoes
- 2 red bell peppers
- 4 golden apples, cored
- 2 oranges
- 2 medium carrots
- 4 large beets

Directions:

1. Wash the vegetables and fruits.
2. Chop the bell peppers and sweet potatoes into chunks. Core the apples and chop into chunks.
3. Peel the oranges and separate the segments.
4. Juice together sweet potatoes, bell peppers, apples, oranges, carrots, and beets in the juicer.
5. Pour the juice into glasses and serve with crushed ice.

Papaya and Guava Juice

Serves: 2

Ingredients:

- 1 teaspoon lemon juice
- 2 teaspoons pure maple syrup or brown sugar or stevia
- 2 sprigs parsley
- 2-inch piece ginger
- 1 ½ cups ripe papaya chunks
- 2 guavas
- 2 cups water

Directions:

1. Wash ginger, parsley, and guavas. Peel and slice ginger. Chop parsley. Chop guava into pieces.
2. Blend together guava, ginger, parsley, papaya, and water in a blender until smooth.
3. Strain the juice. Add lemon juice and sweetener and stir.
4. Pour into glasses and serve with crushed ice.

The Pepper Magic Drink

Serves: 2

Ingredients:

- 2 bunches spinach
- 4 sticks celery
- 2 red bell peppers
- 2 kiwis

Directions:

1. Wash the vegetables and kiwis.
2. Chop spinach, celery, and bell pepper into pieces.
3. Peel the kiwis and chop into chunks.
4. Juice together spinach, celery, bell peppers, and kiwis in a juicer and extract the juice.
5. Pour into glasses and serve with ice if desired.

Berry and Apple Juice

Serves: 2

Ingredients:

- 10 large strawberries, hulled
- 6 stalks celery
- 4 apples, cored
- 3 cups blueberries
- 2 carrots
- 4 inches fresh ginger, peeled
- 1 cucumber

Directions:

1. Wash all the fruits and vegetables. Chop celery into 2-inch pieces. Chop apples, cucumber and carrots into chunks.
2. Juice together strawberries, celery, apple, blueberries, carrot, ginger, and cucumber in a juicer.
3. Pour into glasses. Serve with crushed ice.

Mixed Berry Juice

Serves: 2

Ingredients:

- ½ cup raspberries
- ½ cup blueberries
- ½ cup strawberries
- ½ cup blackberries
- 2 apples, cored
- 4 oranges
- ½ cup water if required

Directions:

1. Peel the oranges and separate them into segments.
2. Juice together apples and oranges in the juicer.
3. Pour the juice into the blender. Add all the berries and blend until smooth. If the juice is very thick, add some water if required and blend until smooth.
4. Pour into glasses and serve with ice.

Chapter 5:

Juices for Happy State of Mind

Even though happiness is a state of mind, it is influenced by different physiological factors. From the diet you follow to your physical health different factors are at play. Your mental health and happiness are compromised when you aren't physically healthy and vice versa. The simplest way to retain the happiness quotient is by consuming a diet that is nutritious, light, keeps the blues away, and keeps you active. The quickest and efficient means to do this is by increasing the intake of fruits and vegetables. Some common fruits and veggies that can make you happy are bananas, berries, leafy greens, apples, and oranges. Add all these ingredients to your diet by using the delicious and happiness-inducing juices discussed in this chapter.

Orange and Mango Juice

Serves: 2

Ingredients:

- 2 oranges
- 6 large strawberries
- 2 handfuls spinach
- 6 Romaine lettuce leaves
- 1 mango, peeled, deseeded
- 2 carrots, peeled
- 2 small cucumbers, peeled

Directions:

1. Wash all the fruits and vegetables. Peel the oranges and separate the segments.
2. Chop mango, carrots, cucumbers, and strawberries into chunks.
3. Add oranges, strawberries, spinach, lettuce, mango, carrots, and cucumbers into a blender. Blend until you get a smooth mixture.
4. Strain the juice and pour into tall glasses.

Strawberry, Carrot, and Mango Juice

Serves: 2

Ingredients:

- 2 cups strawberries, fresh or frozen
- 1 mango, peeled
- 15–20 baby carrots
- 2 navel oranges
- 2 cups chilled coconut water

Directions:

1. Wash all the fruits and carrots. Chop mango and carrots into chunks. Peel the oranges and separate the segments.
2. Juice together carrots and oranges in a juicer.
3. Pour the extracted juice into a blender. Add coconut water, strawberries and mango.
4. Blend for 30-40 seconds or until smooth. Add more coconut water if you like the juice diluted.
5. Pour into glasses and serve.

Banana and Mango Juice

Serves: 2

Ingredients:

- 4 cups spinach or dark leafy greens of your choice
- 1 medium mango
- 1 banana
- 3 cups coconut water or water
- 2 cups fresh pineapple chunks

Directions:

1. Wash the fruits and spinach.
2. Peel the mango and banana and cut into pieces.
3. Add spinach, mango, banana, pineapple and water into a blender. Blend until smooth.
4. Strain the juice.
5. Pour into glasses. Serve with crushed ice.

Pineapple and Avocado Juice

Serves: 2

Ingredients:

- 2 cups water
- 2 green tea bags
- 2 cups baby kale or any other greens of your choice
- 2 cups pineapple chunks
- 2 cups cilantro
- 2 cups cucumber
- Juice of 2 lemons
- 1 avocado, peeled, pitted
- 2 tablespoons freshly grated ginger

Directions:

1. Prepare the green tea using 2 cups water and green tea bags following the directions given on the package.
2. Wash all the vegetables and avocado.
3. Chop the avocado into pieces.
4. Add kale, pineapple, cilantro, cucumber, lemon juice, avocado, ginger, and about 1 cup of the green tea into a blender and blend until smooth.
5. Strain the juice. Stir in remaining green tea.

6. Pour into glasses and serve with crushed ice.

Avocado and Tomato Juice

Serves: 2

Ingredients:

- 1 cup chopped tomatoes
- ¼ avocado
- 1 small cucumber
- 2/3 cup spinach
- Juice of a lemon
- 1 teaspoon cocoa
- Sweetener of your choice to taste

Directions:

1. Wash avocado and all the vegetables.
2. Chop avocado and cucumber into chunks.
3. Add tomatoes, avocado, cocoa, cucumber, spinach, and about 1 cup water into a blender.
4. Blend until smooth. Strain the juice. Add lemon juice and sweetener, and stir.
5. Pour into glasses and serve with crushed ice.

Chapter 6:

Juices to Slow Down Aging

Different nutrients can improve your skin. They can also reduce the signs of aging. So, forget about splurging on expensive cosmetics and other items and instead, focus on increasing the intake of wholesome and healthy fruits and vegetables. If you want supple, youthful, and glowing skin and want to say goodbye to wrinkles, then focus on consuming foods rich in antioxidants. Oxidative stress and damage are the leading cause of aging. Try the different recipes given in this chapter to reduce the signs of aging while providing your skin with the nutrients it needs to stay healthy.

Red Cabbage Juice

Serves: 1

Ingredients:

- 1 cup plums or raspberries
- 2 cups shredded red cabbage
- 1 zucchini

- 2 large purple carrots or sweet potatoes

Directions:

1. Wash all the vegetables and fruits. Pit the plums if using.
2. Chop the zucchini and carrots into chunks. Peel the sweet potatoes if using and chop into chunks.
3. Place carrots or sweet potato, red cabbage, plums, and zucchini in the juicer and extract the juice.
4. You can also add all the ingredients into a blender and blend until smooth. Strain the juice if you are blending them in a blender.
5. Pour into a glass and serve.

Anti-aging Citrus Juice to Reduce Wrinkles

Serves: 2

Ingredients:

- 5–6 mandarin oranges
- ½ grapefruit

- 3 oranges
- Agave syrup to taste (optional)

Directions:

1. Cut the oranges, grapefruit and mandarin oranges into 2 halves horizontally.
2. Squeeze the juice of all the citrus fruits using a citrus juicer.
3. You can also peel the citrus fruits and separate them into segments. Place them in a juicer and extract the juice.
4. Stir well and pour into glasses. Add agave nectar to taste if desired and serve with ice if desired.

Pink Juice for Anti-aging

Serves: 1

Ingredients:

- 1 cup red grapes
- 2 beetroots
- 2 sticks celery
- 2 large carrots

Directions:

1. Wash all the vegetables and grapes. Use the beet greens if you prefer.
2. Chop the beetroots and carrots into chunks. Cut the celery into about 2-inch pieces.
3. Place carrots, beetroots, grapes, and celery in the juicer and extract the juice. You can also put all the ingredients into a blender and blend until smooth. Strain the juice if you are blending them in a blender.
4. Pour into a glass and serve with ice.

Apple and Blueberry Juice

Serves: 1

Ingredients:

- 1 apple, cored
- 1 cup blueberries

Directions:

1. Wash the fruits and core the apple. Peel the apple if desired and chop into chunks.

2. Place blueberries and apple in a blender and blend until smooth. Add ice and blend once again.
3. Pour into a glass and serve. Do drink the juice as soon as it is made. Keeping it for long will make the juice jelly-like.

Pomegranate and Mint Juice

Serves: 2

Ingredients:

- 1 cup packed mint leaves
- 2 whole pomegranates

Directions:

1. Wash the pomegranates and cut them open. Remove the seeds. Discard the skin and membranes.
2. Place pomegranate seeds and mint leaves in a blender. Give short pulses until you get juice. The seeds should not be ground else you will end up with slightly bitter juice. But then some seeds may be broken while pulsing.

3. Pour the juice into a strainer and strain the juice.
4. Pour the juice into glasses. Garnish with some mint leaves and serve.

Anti-aging Green Monster Juice

Serves: 2

Ingredients:

- 4 large apples, cored
- 1 cucumber
- 8 medium carrots
- 15-16 kale leaves, discard hard stem and ribs
- 2 teaspoons sea buckthorn (olivello) juice (optional)
- ½ cup plain yogurt, beaten
- Ice cubes as required

Directions:

1. Wash apples and vegetables. Chop cucumber, apples, and carrots into chunks.
2. Juice together apples, kale, cucumber and carrots in the juicer.
3. Add sea buckthorn juice and yogurt and stir.

4. Pour into glasses and serve with ice.

Chapter 7:

Juices for Bone Health

Unless your skeleton is strong and resilient, your overall health is compromised. So, taking care of your bones cannot be overlooked. Bones are predominantly made of calcium phosphate and collagen. As with any other body part, even old bone cells are shed, and new ones are created as a replacement. With age, the body's ability to do this slows down resulting in weak and brittle bones. Well, movement becomes a challenge if your bones aren't strong enough. Now, the good news is that juicing is a great way to improve bone health while obtaining a variety of other helpful nutrients. Some common foods for stronger and healthier bones include berries, leafy greens, celery, and cucumbers. Use the different recipes given in this chapter to improve your bone health.

Ease Your Joints Juice

Serves: 1

Ingredients:

- 1 cup chopped fresh pineapple
- ½ cup red grapes
- 1 inch fresh ginger root
- ¼ cup cherries, pitted
- ½ large carrot
- 1 inch fresh turmeric root

Directions:

1. Wash all the fruits and vegetables.
2. Chop carrot into chunks.
3. Place pineapple, grapes, ginger, cherries, carrot, and turmeric in a juicer and extract the juice.
4. You can also put all the ingredients into a blender and blend until smooth. Strain the juice if you are blending them in a blender.
5. Pour into a glass and serve with ice.

Grapefruit Juice

Serves: 2

Ingredients:

- 4 grapefruits
- 4 oranges

Directions:

1. Wash the grapefruits and oranges. Cut them into 2 halves horizontally.
2. Juice them in a citrus juicer. You can also squeeze the grapefruits and oranges with your hand.
3. To juice the citrus fruits in a juicer: Peel the grapefruits and oranges. Separate the segments.
4. Place grapefruits and oranges in a juicer and extract the juice.
5. Pour into glasses. Serve with crushed ice.

All Green Juice

Serves: 2

Ingredients:

- 8 sticks celery
- 1 head broccoli
- 2 cucumbers
- ½ lemon

Directions:

1. Wash all the vegetables and chop them into chunks. Peel the lemon.
2. Juice together celery, broccoli, cucumbers, and lemon in the juicer and extract the juice.
3. You can also put them all in a blender, adding some water and blend until smooth. Strain the juice if you are blending them in a blender.
4. Pour into glasses and serve.

Anti-inflammatory Tonic

Serves: 2

Ingredients:

- 2 inches fresh turmeric
- 1 inch fresh ginger
- 1 lemon
- 8 carrots
- 2 oranges
- 6 sticks celery

Directions:

1. Wash all the vegetables and oranges.
2. Peel the lemon and cut into halves or quarters.
3. Chop carrots into chunks. Peel the oranges and separate the segments.
4. Cut celery into 2 inch pieces.
5. Add turmeric, ginger, lemon, carrots, oranges, and celery into a juicer.
6. Extract the juice. Pour into glasses and serve with crushed ice.

Spinach and Kale Green Juice

Serves: 2

Ingredients:

- 1 bunch kale leaves, discard hard stems and ribs
- 1 bunch spinach
- 1 ½ lemons, peeled
- 4 oranges
- 2 green apples, cored

Directions:

1. Wash all the vegetables and fruits. Chop apples into chunks. Chop spinach into large pieces. Peel the oranges and separate out the segments.
2. Add kale, spinach, lemons, oranges and apples into a juicer and extract the juice.
3. Pour into 2 glasses.
4. Serve with crushed ice.

Anti-inflammatory Citrus Juice

Serves: 2

Ingredients:

- 2 oranges
- 2 lemons
- 4 slices fresh pineapple
- 1 inch piece fresh ginger
- 2 ruby grapefruits
- 2 sticks celery

Directions:

1. Wash all the fruits and vegetables. Slice the celery as well. Cut the citrus fruits into 2 halves horizontally. Extract the juice from the citrus fruits using a citrus juicer. You can also squeeze the juice using your hands.
2. Place celery, ginger, pineapple, and some of the extracted juice in a blender and blend until smooth. Strain the juice. Stir in the remaining juice.
3. Pour into 2 glasses and serve.

Tomato and Celery Juice

Serves: 2

Ingredients:

- 4 tomatoes
- ½ lemon, peeled
- 4 stalks celery
- Freshly ground pepper to taste
- A dash Tabasco sauce
- A dash Worcestershire sauce

Directions:

1. Wash the vegetables. Chop tomatoes and celery into chunks.
2. Add tomatoes, lemon, and celery into a juicer and extract the juice.
3. Stir in pepper, Tabasco sauce, and Worcestershire sauce.
4. Pour into glasses and serve with ice.

Juice to Prevent Osteoporosis

Serves: 2

Ingredients:

- 8 stalks celery
- 1 head broccoli
- ½ lemon, peeled
- 2 cucumbers

Directions:

1. Wash all the vegetables.
2. Chop celery, broccoli, and cucumber into chunks.
3. Add celery, broccoli, lemon, and cucumbers into a juicer and extract the juice.
4. Pour into glasses and serve with ice.

Chapter 8:

Antioxidant Juices

Antioxidants help your body reduce oxidative stress and also prevent inflammation and other issues. This chapter has some of the best recipes you can use to increase the number of antioxidants in your body.

Cranberry Cucumber Juice

Serves: 2

Ingredients:

- 2 beetroots
- 12–15 cranberries
- 1 cucumber
- 1 cup chopped cilantro
- 1 tomato
- 1/8 teaspoon cayenne pepper
- 1/8 teaspoon salt

Directions:

1. Wash the vegetables and cranberries.
2. Chop cucumber, tomatoes, and beets into chunks.
3. Place beetroots, cranberries, cucumber, cilantro, and tomato in a juicer and extract the juice.
4. Pour juice into glasses and serve with crushed ice.

Cranberry Apple Juice

Serves: 2

Ingredients:

- 1 ½ cups cranberries
- 4 apples
- 6 carrots

Directions:

1. Wash the fruits and carrots. Chop apples and carrots into chunks.
2. Juice together cranberries, apples and carrots in a juicer.
3. Pour into glasses and serve with crushed ice.

Strawberry Watermelon Juice

Serves: 2

Ingredients:

- 3 cups watermelon cubes, deseeded
- 15-18 large strawberries, hulled
- 2 tablespoons lemon juice or to taste
- ½ cup water
- Ice cubes, as required

Directions:

1. Wash the strawberries and chop into chunks.
2. Add strawberries and watermelon cubes into a blender and blend until smooth.
3. Add water and lemon juice and blend again.
4. Strain the juice if you do not prefer the strawberry seeds and pour into glasses. Add ice cubes and serve.

Kiwi Juice

Serves: 2

Ingredients:

- 1 cup cubed fresh pineapple
- 6 kiwis
- 1 inch fresh ginger
- 4 red apples, cored
- 2 sticks celery
- 1 cup fresh mint leaves

Directions:

1. Wash the fruits and vegetables.
2. Chop the apples into chunks.
3. Peel kiwi's and cut into pieces. Cut celery into 2-inch pieces
4. Add pineapple, kiwis, ginger, mint leaves, apples, and celery into a juicer and extract the juice.
5. Pour the extracted juice into glasses and serve with ice.

Chapter 9:

Colon Cleansing Juices

The colon, also known as the large intestine or large bowel, plays a crucial role in digesting, utilizing, and excreting the food consumed. Cleaning the colon regularly is good for removing toxins from the gastrointestinal tract. This helps improve your energy levels, immune functioning, and reduces the risk of problems such as arthritis and hypertension too. Consuming colorful fruits and vegetables is an efficient means to cleanse and strengthen the colon. For instance, orange and yellow-colored fruits and veggies such as mangoes, oranges, and carrots improve digestive health along with immune functioning, and skin and eye health. The different recipes given in this chapter will help achieve this goal.

Cleansing Green Juice

Serves: 2

Ingredients:

- 1 ½ cucumbers
- 1 gala apple, cored
- ¼ lemon
- 2 leaves hearts of Romaine lettuce
- 1 stalk celery

Directions:

1. Wash the vegetables and apples.
2. Chop cucumber into pieces. Stack the lettuce leaves and roll it up. Cut celery into 2-inch pieces.
3. Peel the lemon. Chop into pieces.
4. Place cucumber, apple, lemon, lettuce leaves, and celery in a juicer and extract the juice.
5. Divide the juice into glasses and serve with ice.

Beetroot Juice

Serves: 1

Ingredients:

- 1 cup grapes
- 3 beets
- 1 teaspoon lemon juice or to taste
- A pinch salt

Directions:

1. Wash the beetroot and grapes.
2. Chop the beets into chunks.
3. Place grapes and beets in a juicer and extract the juice.
4. Pour into a glass. Add lemon juice and salt and stir.

Prune Juice for Constipation Relief

Serves: 1

Ingredients:

- 6 prunes
- 1 teaspoon honey
- 1 tablespoon lemon juice
- 1 cup water

Directions:

1. Soak prunes in water for 30 minutes.
2. Add prunes along with the soaked water into a blender. Blend until smooth.
3. Pour into a glass. Add honey and lemon juice and stir.
4. Place the glass in the refrigerator for an hour and serve.

Pineapple and Kiwi Juice

Serves: 2

Ingredients:

- 2 cups cubed fresh pineapple
- 2 kiwis
- 1 cup diced papaya
- 1 cup fresh coconut water

Directions:

1. Peel kiwis and chop into chunks.
2. Blend together pineapple, kiwi, papaya, and coconut water in a blender until smooth.
3. This juice is to be had in the morning before eating or drinking anything.

Morning Juice

Serves: 2

Ingredients:

- 1 grapefruit

- 4 stalks celery
- 6 radishes
- 2 inches fresh ginger
- 2 lemons
- 1 cucumber
- 2 red apples, cored

Directions:

1. Wash all the fruits and vegetables.
2. Chop celery, radish, ginger, apples, and cucumbers into chunks.
3. Peel the lemons and grapefruit but make sure to retain some of the pith. Separate the grapefruit segments.
4. Cut the lemons into halves.
5. Add grapefruit, celery, radishes, ginger, lemons, cucumber, and apples into a juicer and extract the juice.
6. Serve with ice.

Beet Juice to Relieve Constipation

Serves: 2

Ingredients:

- 6 beets
- 4 carrots
- 2 teaspoons chia seeds or flaxseeds
- 4 green apples, cored
- 2 cups spinach

Directions:

1. Wash all the vegetables and apples.
2. Chop beets, apples, and carrots into chunks.
3. Juice together beets, apples, spinach, and carrots in a juicer.
4. Pour into glasses. Add a teaspoon of chia seeds into each glass and stir.
5. Serve.

Apple and Kiwi Punch

Serves: 2

Ingredients:

- 6 kiwis
- 2 cups spinach
- 4 green apples
- Juice of a lemon

Directions:

1. Wash the fruit and vegetables.
2. Peel kiwis and apples and chop into chunks
3. Add kiwis, apples, spinach and some water into a blender and blend until smooth. Add lemon juice and stir.
4. Serve with ice.

Green Orange Bowel Booster

Serves: 2

Ingredients:

- 6 oranges
- 4 cups spinach
- 4 green apples, cored

Directions:

1. Wash fruit and spinach.
2. Peel and chop apples into chunks.
3. Cut the oranges into 2 halves. Squeeze the orange juice with a citrus juicer.
4. Place apples, spinach, and orange juice in a blender and blend until smooth.
5. Pour into glasses and serve with ice.

Chapter 10:

Detox Juices

Detoxification is a biological process that keeps running in the background all the time to eliminate waste from the body. Toxic by-products created due to cellular metabolism and regular body functions are removed along with any environmental toxins present within during a detox. The organs responsible for it include the liver, kidneys, colon, lungs and skin. The simplest way to support this function is by consuming nutrient-dense fruits and vegetables (Yu-Jie Zhang et al., 2015). The different detox juice recipes given here will quicken this process and its efficiency while improving your health.

Green Detox Juice

Serves: 1

Ingredients:

- ½ green apple, cored
- ½ large English cucumber

- 1 tablespoon fresh lemon juice
- A large handful parsley with stems and leaves
- 1 cup packed baby spinach
- ½ inch fresh ginger

Directions:

1. Wash the apple and vegetables.
2. Chop the apple and cucumber into chunks. Tear the parsley and spinach into large pieces.
3. Juice together the apples, cucumber, spinach, parsley, and ginger in the juicer. You can also put all the ingredients into a blender and blend until smooth. Strain the juice if you are blending them in a blender.
4. Add lemon juice and stir.
5. Pour into a glass and serve.

The Newbie

Serves: 2–3

Ingredients:

- 2 cups torn lettuce leaves
- 10 celery stalks
- 2 cucumbers

- 2 green apples, cored
- Juice of 2 lemons or to taste

Directions:

1. Wash the apple and vegetables.
2. Chop the apple, celery, and cucumber into chunks.
3. Juice together the apples, cucumber, lettuce, and celery in the juicer. You can also put all the ingredients into a blender and blend until smooth. Strain the juice if you are blending them in a blender.
4. Add lemon juice and stir.
5. Pour into glasses and serve.

The Detoxer

Serves: 1

Ingredients:

- 1 cucumber
- A small bunch cilantro, with leaves and stems
- A small bunch parsley, with leaves and stems
- 2 kale leaves
- 2 tablespoons fresh lemon juice or to taste

- 4 sticks celery
- 2 Swiss chard leaves
- A pinch cayenne pepper (optional)
- 2 inches fresh ginger, peeled

Directions:

1. Wash all vegetables.
2. Chop the cucumbers and celery into chunks. Chop the greens into big pieces with its stem.
3. Add cucumber, celery, ginger, and greens into a juicer and extract the juice. You can also put the ingredients into a blender and blend until smooth. Strain the juice if you are blending them in a blender.
4. Add lemon juice and cayenne pepper and stir.
5. Pour into a glass and serve.

Green Beet Juice

Serves: 2

Ingredients:

- 2 beets
- 8 kale leaves
- 8 sticks celery

- 2 cucumbers
- Juice of 2 lemons

Directions:

1. Wash all the vegetables. Chop beets, celery, and cucumber into chunks.
2. Tear up the kale leaves.
3. Add cucumber, celery, and kale into a juicer and extract the juice. You can also put all the ingredients in a blender and blend until smooth. Strain the juice if you are blending them in a blender.
4. Add lemon juice and stir.
5. Pour into glasses and serve.

Green Cucumber Juice

Serves: 1

Ingredients:

- 1 small cucumber
- A small bunch cilantro, with leaves and stems
- A small bunch parsley, with leaves and stems
- 2 kale leaves
- 1 tablespoon fresh lime juice or to taste

- ½ large green apple, cored

Directions:

1. Wash all the vegetables and apple.
2. Chop the cucumbers and apple into chunks. Chop the parsley and cilantro into large pieces. Tear the kale leaves.
3. Add cucumber, apple, and greens into a juicer and extract the juice. You can also add all the ingredients into a blender and blend until smooth. Strain the juice if you are blending them in a blender.
4. Add lime juice and stir.
5. Pour into a glass and serve.

Chapter 11:

Juices for the Digestive system

The organs that make up our system are the mouth, stomach, small intestine, pancreas, liver, gallbladder, colon, rectum, and anus. If this entire system is not working properly, it can result in diarrhea, constipation, hemorrhoids, heartburn, ulcers, gallstones, stomach flu, lactose intolerance, Crohn's disease, celiac disease, and a variety of other conditions. Consuming wholesome fruits and vegetables is a great way to strengthen the functioning of the digestive system and improve its health (Annett Klinder et al., 2016). You can achieve all these benefits by adding the fruit juices discussed in this chapter to your diet.

Digestion-soothing Juice

Serves: 2

Ingredients:

- 1 ½ cucumbers
- 2 small fennel bulbs with fronds
- ½ small bunch fresh cilantro
- Juice of ½ lime
- 1 Granny Smith apple, cored
- A pinch salt
- 2 sticks celery
- 1 ½ inches fresh ginger

Directions:

1. Wash the apple and vegetables.
2. Chop apples, cucumbers, fennel, fennel fronds, cilantro, and celery into large pieces.
3. Add apple, ginger cilantro, celery, fennel fronds, and fennel bulbs into a juicer and extract the juice.
4. Add lime juice and salt and stir. Serve with ice.

Gut Healing Juice

Serves: 1

Ingredients:

- 2 cups fresh pineapple cubes
- 1 inch fresh ginger
- 3 sticks celery
- 1 small cucumber
- ½ lemon, peeled
- ½ bunch collard greens
- A small bunch parsley
- 1 large handful fresh spinach

Directions:

1. Wash all the vegetables.
2. Chop cucumber and celery into chunks. Chop spinach, parsley, and collard greens into large pieces.
3. Place celery, spinach, cucumber, lemon, ginger, parsley, collard greens, and pineapple in a juicer to extract the juice.
4. Pour into a glass and serve with crushed ice.

Juice for Constipation Relief

Serves: 2

Ingredients:

- ½ large bunch watercress
- 4 celery stalks
- 2 cups chopped fresh pineapple
- 2 inches fresh ginger

Directions:

1. Wash the vegetables.
2. Chop celery and watercress into large pieces.
3. Juice together watercress, pineapple, celery, and ginger in a juicer.
4. Pour into glasses and serve with ice.

Juice for Upset Stomach

Serves: 1

Ingredients:

- ½ apple, cored

- 1 small cucumber
- ½ beet
- ½ stalk celery
- 1-inch ginger
- ½ tablespoon apple cider vinegar
- A small bunch fresh mint

Directions:

1. Wash apple and vegetables.
2. Chop cucumber, beet, celery and apple into chunks. Pick the mint leaves from the bunch.
3. Juice together apple, celery, mint, beet, carrots and cucumber in a juicer. Add apple cider vinegar and stir. Taste the juice and dilute it with water if desired.
4. Serve.

Carrot Apple Juice for Diarrhea

Serves: 2

Ingredients:

- 2 carrots
- 1 cup thyme leaves
- 1 apple, cored

- A pinch salt

Directions:

1. Wash carrots, thyme, and apple. Peel the carrots and apple and chop into chunks.
2. Add carrots, thyme, and apple into a blender and blend until smooth.
3. Strain the juice if desired. Add salt and stir. Serve with ice.

Cucumber Juice for Indigestion and Constipation Relief

Serves: 2

Ingredients:

- 2 small cucumbers
- 1 apple, cored
- 2 cups chopped spinach
- 2 cups celery leaves

Directions:

1. Wash all the vegetables and apple. Peel the apple and cucumbers and chop into chunks.
2. Add cucumbers, apple, spinach, and celery into a blender and blend until smooth.
3. Serve with ice.

Chapter 12:

Juices for Anemia

Anemia occurs when the count of red blood cells is too low. This, in turn, results in insufficient supply of oxygen to cells for optimal functioning because of low count of iron rich protein known as hemoglobin. This is a chronic health condition and when left unregulated results in several other problems. Increasing your intake of fruits and vegetables is the surest way to tackle anemia and reduce its risk (Bishwajit Ghose and Sanni Yaya, 2018). Some common fruit and vegetables needed to tackle anemia include pomegranate, kale, colored peppers, avocado, spinach, and banana. The different recipes given here will come in handy to tackle anemia.

Parsley Juice

Serves: 2

Ingredients:

- 2 bunches parsley
- 1 orange

- 1 green apple
- 1 lemon
- 2 cucumbers

Directions:

1. Wash all the fruits and vegetables.
2. Peel the cucumbers and apple and chop into chunks. Peel the orange and separate the segments. Peel the lemon and cut into 2 halves.
3. Juice together parsley, orange, apple, lemon, and cucumbers in a juicer.
4. Serve with ice.

Beet, Orange, and Carrot Juice

Serves: 2–3

Ingredients:

- 2 beets
- 12 oranges
- 2 carrots

Directions:

1. Wash the vegetables and oranges.

2. Peel the oranges and separate the segments. Chop beets and carrots into chunks.
3. Juice together oranges, beets, and carrots in a juicer. You can also add all the ingredients into a blender and blend until smooth.
4. Strain the juice and serve.

High Iron Vegetable Juice

Serves: 2

Ingredients:

- 4 cups baby spinach
- 2 medium beets with leaves
- 2 small cucumbers
- 6 kale leaves
- 2 tomatoes
- 4 carrots
- 2 small leaves Swiss chard
- 14–15 sprigs parsley

Directions:

1. Wash all the vegetables. Chop cucumbers, carrots, tomatoes, and beets into chunks. Chop the greens into large pieces.

2. Juice together spinach, beets, beet greens, cucumbers, kale, tomatoes, carrots, Swiss chard, and parsley in a juicer.
3. Pour into glasses and serve with ice.

Iron Boost

Serves: 2

Ingredients:

- 1 cucumber
- 2 cups Romaine lettuce
- 2 green apples, cored
- 4 sticks celery
- 2 cups broccoli florets
- Juice of a lime

Directions:

1. Wash the vegetables and apples.
2. Chop cucumber, celery, and carrots into chunks. Tear the lettuce leaves.
3. Add broccoli, celery, lettuce, apples, and cucumber into a juicer and extract the juice. Stir in lime juice.
4. Pour into glasses and serve with ice.

Blueberry and Spinach Juice

Serves: 1

Ingredients:

- 1 cup fresh blueberries
- 1 Fuji apple, cored
- 1 cup fresh spinach leaves

Directions:

1. Wash fruit and spinach.
2. Chop apple into chunks. Cut the spinach leaves into large pieces.
3. Add apple, spinach, and blueberries into a juicer and extract the juice.
4. You can also blend together all the ingredients in a blender until smooth.
5. Strain the juice and serve with ice.

Iron Boosting Sweet and Tart Green Juice

Serves: 2

Ingredients:

- 1 banana
- 1 Asian pear, cored
- Juice of 4 small lemons
- Juice of 4 small limes
- ½ cup water
- 1 Granny Smith apple, cored
- 2 cups chopped spinach
- Honey to taste

Directions:

1. Wash the fruits and vegetables. Peel and chop the apple and pear into chunks. Peel and chop bananas.
2. Add banana, pear, lemon juice, lime juice, water, apple, spinach, and honey into a blender and blend until smooth.
3. Pour into glasses and serve.

Leafy Greens

Serves: 2

Ingredients:

- 16 spinach leaves
- 4 celery stalks
- 2 beets
- 2 apples
- 4 kale leaves

Directions:

1. Wash all the vegetables and apples. Chop beets, celery, and apples into chunks. Chop the greens into large pieces.
2. Add beets, greens, celery, and apples into a juicer and extract the juice.

Chapter 13:

Juices for Lowering Blood Pressure

The pressure with which blood pushes against the walls of the arteries is known as the blood pressure. Usually, it rises and reduces throughout the day. If it's higher than the normal range of 120/80 mmHG, it's known as hypertension. This is a risk factor for other health conditions such as heart diseases, strokes, and heart attacks. Potassium, flavonoids, and other helpful nutrients found in fruits and vegetables help reduce and regulate blood pressure (Aedin Cassidy et al., 2011). Adding berries, bananas, kiwis, melons, and leafy greens is a good idea. Ensure that your body obtains its daily dose of nutrients along with other helpful plant compounds needed to regulate blood pressure by using the recipes given in this chapter.

Green Juice

Serves: 1

Ingredients:

- ½ green apple, cored
- 2 celery sticks
- ½ lemon, peeled
- 1 cucumber
- ½ large bunch parsley
- 2 inches fresh ginger

Directions:

1. Wash the vegetables and apple. Chop apple, celery, and cucumber into chunks.
2. Chop parsley into large pieces.
3. Juice together apple, celery, lemon, cucumber, parsley, and ginger in a juicer.

Pineapple and Celery Juice

Serves: 2

Ingredients:

- 2 cups chopped pineapple
- 1 large zucchini
- 1 cucumber
- 2 cups celery leaves
- 2 large bunches parsley
- 2 inches fresh ginger

Directions:

1. Wash the vegetables.
2. Chop zucchini and cucumber into chunks.
3. Add pineapple, zucchini, cucumber, celery, parsley, and ginger into a juicer. Extract the juice.
4. Pour the extracted juice into glasses and serve with ice.

Beet, Carrot, Pineapple, and Orange Juice

Serves: 1–2

Ingredients:

- 4 small beets
- 3 cups chopped fresh pineapple
- 2 inches fresh ginger
- 4 oranges
- 8 large carrots

Directions:

1. Wash the vegetables and oranges.
2. Chop beets and carrots into chunks. Peel the oranges and separate the segments.
3. Juice together beets, pineapple, ginger, oranges, and carrots in a juicer.
4. You can also blend together all the ingredients in a blender until smooth.
5. Pour into glasses and serve with ice.

Pear and Zucchini Juice

Serves: 2

Ingredients:

- 2 pears, cored
- 5 sticks celery
- 1 grapefruit
- 4 zucchinis
- 2 large bunches cilantro
- 2 inches fresh turmeric

Directions:

1. Wash the vegetables and fruits.
2. Chop pears, celery, and zucchini into chunks. Peel the grapefruit. Separate the segments.
3. Add pears, grapefruit, zucchini, cilantro, turmeric, and celery, into a juicer and extract the juice.
4. Pour into glasses and serve with ice.

Beet, Carrot, Pineapple, and Orange Juice

Serves: 1

Ingredients:

- 1 small beet
- 2 cups chopped pineapple with core
- 2 large carrots
- 1 medium orange

Directions:

1. Wash the beet, carrots, and orange.
2. Chop carrots and beet into chunks. Peel the orange and separate the segments.
3. Juice together beet, pineapple, carrots, and orange in a juicer.
4. Serve with ice.

Tropical Carrot Juice

Serves: 2

Ingredients:

- ½ cup chopped carrots
- ½ cup chopped fresh pineapple
- Water, as required
- ½ cup cubed mango
- ½ inch fresh ginger

Directions:

1. Peel and grate the ginger.
2. Add carrots, pineapple, water, mango, and ginger into a blender and blend until smooth.
3. Strain if desired and serve.

Chapter 14:

Anti-inflammatory Juices

The immune system's response to any injury or infection is known as inflammation. In regulated doses, this is an extremely helpful reaction. However, when left unchecked it results in chronic inflammation that's a precursor to other chronic health conditions including hypertension, poor cardiovascular health, arthritis, and so on. To tackle inflammation, increasing the intake of antioxidant foods along with other anti-inflammatory foods is needed. Fruits and vegetables serve this function. Some common ingredients that tackle inflammation include berries, avocados, carrots, kale, oranges, and spinach. By using the fruit and veggie juice recipes given in this chapter, you can tackle inflammation.

Green Pineapple Juice

Serves: 2

Ingredients:

- 2 cups chopped pineapple
- 4 cups chopped spinach
- 1 large celery stalk
- 2 inches fresh ginger
- 2 medium apples, cored
- ½ small cucumber
- ½ lemon, unpeeled

Directions:

1. Wash the vegetables and apples.
2. Chop celery, apples, and cucumber into chunks.
3. Add apples, celery, pineapple, spinach, ginger, lemon, and cucumber into the juicer and extract the juice.

Carrot, Pineapple, and Turmeric Juice

Serves: 2

Ingredients:

- 8 carrots
- 4 inches fresh turmeric
- 2 cups chopped fresh pineapple
- 1/8 teaspoon black pepper

Directions:

1. Chop carrots into chunks. Cut turmeric into pieces.
2. Add carrots, turmeric, and pineapple into a juicer and extract the juice.
3. Pour into glasses. Add pepper and stir. Pepper helps the body to absorb turmeric which is an excellent anti-inflammatory.
4. Serve.

Orange Tonic

Serves: 2

Ingredients:

- 2 inches fresh turmeric
- 1 inch fresh ginger
- 1 lemon
- 8 carrots
- 2 oranges
- 6 sticks celery

Directions:

1. Wash all the vegetables and oranges.
2. Peel the lemon and cut into halves or quarters.
3. Chop the carrots and celery and chop into chunks. Peel the oranges and separate the segments.
4. Add turmeric, ginger, lemon, carrots, oranges, and celery into a juicer and extract the juice.
5. Pour into glasses and serve with crushed ice.

Cinnamon Spiced Tropical Juice

Serves: 1

Ingredients:

- 1 cucumber
- 7–8 pieces fresh turmeric (3 inches each)
- 1 cup fresh pineapple chunks
- ½ tablespoon ground cinnamon

Directions:

1. Wash cucumber and turmeric.
2. Chop cucumber into chunks.
3. Juice together cucumber, turmeric, and pineapple in a juicer and extract the juice.
4. You can also blend together all the ingredients in a blender until smooth. Strain the juice.
5. Pour into a glass. Add cinnamon and stir well.
6. Serve.

Grape and Kale Juice

Serves: 2

Ingredients:

- ½ lemon
- 2 cups grapes
- 2 inches fresh ginger
- 2 bunches kale

Directions:

1. Wash lemon, grapes, ginger, and kale.
2. Peel the lemon and cut into 2 halves. Chop the kale leaves into large pieces.
3. Place lemon, grapes, ginger, and kale in a juicer and extract the juice.
4. Pour into glasses and serve with ice.

Apple and Fennel Juice

Serves: 1

Ingredients:

- 1 tablespoon lemon juice
- 1 large apple, cored
- 1 cup mint leaves
- ½ fennel bulb
- ½ cucumber
- 2 cups spinach leaves

Directions:

1. Wash the vegetables and apple.
2. Chop the apple, fennel bulb, and cucumber into chunks.
3. Add apple, mint, and spinach into a juicer. Extract the juice.
4. Add lemon juice and stir.
5. Serve with ice.

Blueberry and Apple Juice

Serves: 1

Ingredients:

- 1 large apple, cored
- 1 cup blueberries
- 1 cup spinach leaves
- 2 inches fresh turmeric
- A pinch pepper powder

Directions:

1. Wash the fruits and spinach.
2. Chop the apples into chunks.
3. Juice together apples, blueberries, turmeric, and spinach in the juicer.
4. Add pepper and stir. Pepper helps in better absorption of turmeric.
5. Serve with ice.

Watermelon Juice

Serves: 2

Ingredients:

- 4 cups seedless watermelon chunks
- A handful fresh basil leaves
- Juice of a lime

Directions:

1. Add watermelon, basil, and lime juice into a blender and blend until smooth.
2. Serve with ice.

Chapter 15:

Antioxidant Juices

What are antioxidants? They are phytochemicals found in plants along with vitamins A and C, beta-carotene, and selenium. Your body can produce a few antioxidants but most of the requirement is met through dietary sources. These helpful substances slow down and prevent cellular damage caused by free radicals. Free radicals are unstable molecules created as a reaction to different environmental and other pressures within the body. If these free radicals aren't eliminated, it results in oxidative stress associated with inflammation, heart diseases, arthritis, immune problems, and even cancer. These problems can be tackled by increasing the intake of antioxidants (V. Lobo et al., 2010). Apart from this, antioxidants slow down aging, promote cognitive functioning, improve mental health, and increase energy levels. The antioxidant juices given in this chapter will tackle free radicals and improve your health and wellbeing.

Cranberry and Pomegranate Juice

Serves: 2

Ingredients:

- 2 cups cranberries
- ½ inch fresh ginger
- ½ Clementine orange
- ½ apple, cored
- 1/3 Meyer lemon
- ½ cup pomegranate arils
- 1 small clove garlic

Directions:

1. Wash all the fruits and ginger. Peel the orange and separate the segments.
2. Add cranberries, ginger, orange, apple, lemon, pomegranate, and garlic into a juicer and extract the juice.

Cranberry and Cucumber Juice

Serves: 2

Ingredients:

- 2 beets
- 12–15 cranberries
- 1 cucumber
- 1 cup chopped cilantro
- 1 tomato
- 1/8 teaspoon cayenne pepper
- 1/8 teaspoon salt

Directions:

1. Wash the vegetables and cranberries.
2. Chop beets, tomato, and cucumber into chunks.
3. Place beetroots, cranberries, cucumber, cilantro, and tomato in a juicer and extract the juice.
4. Serve with crushed ice.

Antioxidant Power-up Juice

Serves: 2

Ingredients:

- ½ red cabbage
- 1 inch fresh ginger
- 2 beets
- 2 sprigs rosemary
- 4 oranges

Directions:

1. Wash the vegetables and oranges.
2. Chop cabbage and beets into chunks. Peel the oranges and separate into segments.
3. Juice together cabbage, ginger, beets, rosemary, and oranges in a juicer.
4. Serve with ice.

Red Lettuce Juice

Serves: 2

Ingredients:

- 2 heads red lettuce
- 1 inch fresh ginger
- 2 beets
- 2 sprigs basil or thyme
- 4 red carrots

Directions:

1. Wash all the vegetables.
2. Chop carrots and beets into chunks. Chop lettuce into large pieces.
3. Juice together lettuce, ginger, beets, herbs, and carrots in a juicer.
4. Serve with ice.

Sweet Potato and Cabbage Juice

Serves: 2

Ingredients:

- ½ green cabbage
- 1 inch fresh turmeric
- 2 sweet potatoes
- 2 sprigs thyme or rosemary
- 4 carrots

Directions:

1. Wash all the vegetables.
2. Chop cabbage, sweet potato, and carrots into chunks.
3. Juice together cabbage, turmeric, herbs, sweet potatoes, basil, and carrots in a juicer.
4. Serve with ice.

Chapter 16:

Anti-cancer Juices and Juices for Cancer Patients

Cancer refers to a variety of diseases defined by an abnormal development of cells that divide at an uncontrollable rate. These cells then infiltrate and destroy regular and healthy tissue resulting in spread of cancer throughout the body. It is believed to be the second leading cause of death across the world. There exists an undeniable risk between certain types of cancer and the diet consumed. A diet rich in fruits and vegetables helps reduce the risk of the cancers of the mouth, colon, rectum, esophagus, lungs, and stomach (Michael S Donaldson, 2004). Common cancer-fighting fruits and vegetables include relatives, Swiss chard, spinach, chicory, carrots, broccoli, berries, grapefruit, and avocados. Use the different juicing recipes given here to obtain their anti-cancer properties. Those undergoing any treatments to tackle cancer will also benefit from these recipes.

Orange and Cranberry Juice

Serves: 2

Ingredients:

- 6 oranges
- 2 carrots
- 1 cup fresh or frozen cranberries
- 2 teaspoons ground cinnamon

Directions:

1. Wash the vegetables and fruits. Peel the carrots and chop into chunks.
2. Cut the oranges into 2 halves. Squeeze the juice from the oranges with a citrus juicer.
3. Add carrots and cranberries into a blender and blend until smooth.
4. Add orange juice and blend once again until smooth. Stir in cinnamon.
5. Pour into glasses and serve.

Orange, Carrot, and Apple Juice

Serves: 2

Ingredients:

- 6 carrots
- 2 apples, cored
- 2 oranges
- 1 inch fresh ginger

Directions:

1. Wash all the fruits and ginger.
2. Chop apples and carrots into chunks. Peel the oranges and separate the segments.
3. Add apples, carrots, oranges, and ginger into a juicer and extract the juice.
4. Serve with ice.

Breakfast Blend

Serves: 2–3

Ingredients:

- 4 cups chopped strawberries, fresh or frozen
- 2 oranges
- 2 carrots

Directions:

1. Wash fruits and carrots.
2. Chop carrots into chunks. Peel the oranges and separate the segments.
3. Add carrots, oranges, and strawberries into a juicer and extract the juice.
4. Serve with ice.

Blueberry Blast

Serves: 3–4

Ingredients:

- 2 cups blueberries

- 1 cup raspberries
- 2 cups pitted cherries
- 1 cup red grapes

Directions:

1. Wash all the fruit.
2. Juice together berries, cherries, and grapes in a juicer. You can also add all the ingredients into a blender. Blend until smooth.
3. Strain the juice if you are blending in a blender.
4. Serve with ice.

Orange Sunset

Serves: 3–4

Ingredients:

- 4 oranges
- 2 carrots
- 4 kiwis
- 2 cups deseeded, peeled, cubed papaya

Directions:

1. Wash the fruit and carrots.

2. Peel the oranges and separate the segments. Peel carrots and kiwis and chop into chunks.
3. Add oranges, carrots, kiwis, and papaya into a juicer and extract the juice. You can also blend together all the ingredients adding a little water until smooth. Strain the juice if you are blending them.
4. Pour into glasses and serve with ice.

Pink Power

Serves: 2

Ingredients:

- 2 cups pomegranate arils
- 1 cup pitted cherries
- 4 plums, pitted
- 1 cup strawberries

Directions:

1. Wash all the fruit.
2. Juice together pomegranate, cherries, plums and strawberries in a juicer.
3. Serve with ice.

Orange Blast

Serves: 2

Ingredients:

- 4 carrots
- ½ cantaloupe
- 4 apricots, pitted

Directions:

1. Wash all the fruit and carrots.
2. Peel and chop the carrots and cantaloupe into chunks. Discard the seeds of the cantaloupe.
3. Add carrots, cantaloupe, and apricots into a juicer and extract the juice. You can also add the ingredients into a blender and blend until smooth.
4. Strain the juice if you are blending in a blender.
5. Serve with ice.

Cranberry Apple Juice

Serves: 2

Ingredients:

- 4 apples, cored
- 6 carrots
- 1 ½ cups fresh or frozen cranberries

Directions:

1. Wash the carrots and fruit. Peel the apples and carrots and chop into chunks.
2. Add apples, carrots, and cranberries into a blender and blend until smooth.
3. Add a little water while blending if required. Strain if desired and serve with ice.

Ginger Cinnamon Carrot Butternut Squash Juice

(For cancer patients to build immunity)

Serves: 1

Ingredients:

- 1 carrot
- ½ small cucumber
- 1 inch fresh ginger
- 2 cups peeled, deseeded butternut squash
- A pinch Celtic sea salt
- 1 tablespoon lemon juice
- 1/8 teaspoon ground cinnamon or to taste

Directions:

1. Wash all the vegetables. Chop carrot and cucumber into chunks.
2. Juice together carrot, cucumber, ginger, and butternut squash in a juicer.
3. Add salt, lemon juice, and cinnamon and stir.
4. Serve with ice if desired.

Carrot Juice

(For cancer patients with constipation)

Serves: 1

Ingredients:

- 4 oranges
- 4 carrots
- 1 tablespoon lemon juice

Directions:

1. Wash all the carrots and oranges.
2. Chop carrots into chunks. Cut the oranges into 2 halves. Juice the carrots in the juicer.
3. Squeeze the orange juice on a citrus juicer.
4. Combine orange juice, carrot juice and lemon juice in a glass and serve.

Green Machine

(For energy for cancer patients)

Serves: 1

Ingredients:

- 1 medium cucumber
- 2 cups chopped kale
- 2 inches fresh ginger
- 1 cup parsley
- 2 celery stalks
- 2 cups spinach
- Juice of a lemon

Directions:

1. Wash all the vegetables.
2. Chop cucumber into chunks.
3. Juice together cucumber, ginger, greens, and celery in a juicer.
4. Add lemon juice and stir.
5. Serve with ice if desired.

Banana, Apple and Ginger Juice

(For cancer patients with nausea)

Serves: 1

Ingredients:

- 1 banana
- 1 celery stalk
- 1 large apple, cored
- 2 inches fresh ginger
- Water, as required

Directions:

1. Wash all the fruits, celery, and ginger.
2. Peel and chop the banana and apple into chunks. Peel ginger and cut into slices. Chop celery into 2-inch pieces.
3. Add banana, celery, apple, ginger, and water in a blender and blend until smooth.
4. Pour into a glass and serve.

Protein Power Juice

(For cancer patients with loss of appetite or loss of weight)

Serves: 1

Ingredients:

- 1 teaspoon chia seeds
- Honey to taste
- 1 tablespoon cocoa powder
- ½ medium avocado
- 1 tablespoon peanut butter
- ½ cup oat milk

Directions:

1. Add chia seeds, honey, cocoa, avocado, oat milk, and peanut butter into a blender and blend until smooth.
2. Pour into a glass and serve with ice if desired.

Tart Green Juice

(For cancer patients who experience dry mouth)

Serves: 1

Ingredients:

- ¼ banana
- ¼ Asian pear, cored
- Juice of ½ lemon
- Juice of ½ lime
- ¼ Granny Smith apple, cored
- 1 cup spinach
- Honey to taste

Directions:

1. Wash the fruits and spinach. Peel the apple, banana, and pear and chop into chunks.
2. Add banana, apple, pear, spinach, honey, lime juice, lemon juice, and about ½ cup water into a blender and blend until smooth.
3. Serve with ice if desired.

Chapter 17:

Juices for Diabetics

Diabetes is a chronic health condition that hinders the conversion of food into energy by your body. Insulin is a hormone produced by the pancreas to regulate the level of sugar or glucose in the bloodstream. Either the body doesn't produce sufficient insulin or cannot use the insulin available to regulate this. It is a risk factor for other conditions such as cardiovascular disorders, cognitive health problems, skin conditions, and hearing loss too. Higher intake of fruits and vegetables reduces the risk of type-2 diabetes (Ping-Yu Wang et al., 2015). Tackle diabetes and regulate your blood sugar levels by adding some fruits and veggies such as berries, citrus fruits, apples, cherries, leafy greens, and zucchini to your diet. Use the healthy and wholesome fruit and vegetable juice recipes given here to stabilize blood sugar levels.

Bitter Melon Juice

Serves: 1

Ingredients:

- 1 bitter melon
- ½ small cucumber
- 1 tomato

Directions:

1. Wash bitter melon, cucumber, and tomato.
2. Chop bitter melon, cucumber, and tomato into chunks.
3. Add bitter melon, cucumber, and tomato into a blender. Add about ¼ cup of water and blend until smooth.
4. Strain the juice and serve. This recipe should give you about 1/3 cup of juice.
5. Have this juice on an empty stomach in the morning, at least an hour before breakfast.

Apple and Cucumber Juice

Serves: 1

Ingredients:

- 1 cucumber
- 1 apple

Directions:

1. Wash the cucumber and apple. Peel and chop apple and cucumber into chunks.
2. Add cucumber and apple into a juicer and extract the juice. You can also blend together all the ingredients in a blender until smooth. Strain if desired and serve with ice.

Strawberry and Kale Juice

Serves: 1

Ingredients:

- 3 large fresh curly kale leaves
- ¾ cup fresh strawberries

- ½ cup cold water
- 1 inch piece fresh ginger, peeled
- 1 ½ tablespoons lime juice

Directions:

1. Hull and chop the strawberries. Chop the kale leaves into big pieces.
2. Add strawberries, kale, lime juice, cold water, and ginger into a blender.
3. Blend until smooth. Strain the juice and serve with ice.

Cucumber, Pear, Ginger, and Lemon

Serves: 1

Ingredients:

- 1 cucumber
- 1 pear, cored
- 1 inch fresh ginger, peeled
- Juice of ½ lemon

Directions:

1. Wash the cucumber and pear. Peel and chop pear and cucumber into chunks.
2. Add cucumber, pear juice, and ginger into a juicer and extract the juice. Stir in lemon juice.
3. You can also blend together all the ingredients in a blender until smooth. Strain if desired and serve with ice.

Apple and Carrot Juice

Serves: 1

Ingredients:

- 1 ½ green apples, cored
- 1 ½ red apple, cored
- 1 inch fresh ginger
- 2 carrots

Directions:

1. Wash the fruits and vegetables.
2. Chop apples and carrots into chunks.
3. Add apples, ginger, and carrots into a juicer and extract the juice.

Cabbage and Apple Juice

Serves: 1

Ingredients:

- 2 cups chopped chard
- 1 cup chopped kale
- 2 cups chopped cabbage
- 2 apples, cored
- 1 celery stalk
- Juice of ½ lemon

Directions:

1. Wash all the vegetables and apples.
2. Chop celery and apples into chunks.
3. Add greens, cabbage, apples, and celery into a juicer and extract the juice.
4. Stir in lemon juice.
5. Serve with ice if desired.

Mixed Vegetable Juice

Serves: 1

Ingredients:

- 1 carrot
- 1 stalk celery
- ½ cucumber
- 1 tomato
- 1 cup spinach
- 1 cup parsley
- 1 cup lettuce
- 1 cup watercress
- 2 cloves garlic
- 4 Indian gooseberries (amla), pitted

Directions:

1. Wash all the vegetables. Chop carrot, celery, cucumber, and tomatoes into chunks.
2. Add carrot, celery, cucumber, tomato, garlic, Indian gooseberry, and greens into a juicer and extract the juice.
3. Serve with ice.

Chapter 18:

Juices for Pregnancy

During pregnancy, the energy requirements of a woman's body is higher than normal to support the needs of a growing fetus. Avoiding empty calories and replacing it with nutritious food is needed. Consuming fruits and vegetables during pregnancy ensures both mother and the fetus obtain their needed nutrition (Mary M. Murphy et al., 2014). Some highly nutritious fruits and vegetables for a healthy pregnancy include mangoes, lemons, avocados, berries, oranges, apples, and bananas. Try the different recipes given here to obtain your nutritional requirements!

Green Juice

Serves: 1

Ingredients:

- 1 cucumber
- 3 stalks celery
- 3 medium green apples

- 1 inch fresh ginger (optional)

Directions:

1. Wash the vegetables and apples.
2. Chop cucumber, celery, and apples into chunks.
3. Place cucumber, celery, ginger, and green apples in a juicer and extract the juice.
4. Serve with ice.

Green Orange Juice

Serves: 1

Ingredients:

- 4 oranges
- 1 cup spinach
- 6 kale leaves
- 10 stalks asparagus

Directions:

1. Wash the oranges and vegetables.
2. Peel the oranges and separate the segments. Chop kale and asparagus into large pieces.

3. Add oranges, spinach, kale, and asparagus into a juicer and extract the juice.
4. Serve with ice.

Juice to Relieve Morning Sickness

Serves: 1

Ingredients:

- 2 apples, cored
- 1 inch fresh ginger
- 2 celery stalks

Directions:

1. Wash apples, ginger, and celery.
2. Chop celery and apples into chunks.
3. Add apples, ginger, and celery into a juicer and extract the juice.
4. Serve with ice if desired.

Veggie and Fruit Juice

Serves: 1

Ingredients:

- 1 large apple
- 2 small carrots
- 1 orange
- 1 beet
- 1 inch fresh ginger
- ½ tablespoon fresh lemon juice

Directions:

1. Wash all fruits and vegetables.
2. Chop carrots, apple, and beet into chunks.
3. Peel the orange and separate the segments.
4. Add apple, carrots, orange, beet, and ginger into a juicer and extract the juice. Stir in lemon juice.
5. Serve with ice.

Hydrating Blended Juice

Serves: 1

Ingredients:

- 1 cup chopped watermelon
- ½ small cucumber
- 1 inch fresh ginger
- 1 orange
- A handful fresh mint leaves

Directions:

1. Wash cucumber, ginger, orange and mint.
2. Chop cucumber into chunks. Peel and deseed the orange. Remove the membrane of the orange.
3. Add cucumber, orange, ginger, mint, and watermelon into a blender and blend until smooth. Add a little water and blend until smooth.
4. Serve with ice.

Green Juice for Nausea

Serves: 1

Ingredients:

- 4 green apples, cored
- 2 inches fresh ginger
- 2 lemons
- A handful fresh mint leaves

Directions:

1. Wash apples, lemon, ginger and mint.
2. Chop the apples into chunks. Peel lemons and cut into halves.
3. Juice together apples, ginger, lemons, and mint leaves in a juicer.
4. Serve garnished with mint leaves.

Chapter 19:

Juices for Healthy Hair

If you love the idea of a shiny, healthy and thick mane, pay attention to the diet you consume. Humans shed hair follicles daily and that is perfectly fine. If there is excess hair fall, hair looks dull, or if it becomes brittle, it's a sign of an improper diet. If you want healthy hair, increasing the consumption of vegetables and fruits is needed. Consuming plant-based foods such as leafy greens, berries, avocados, and nuts improves hair health (Hayk S. Arakelyan, 2018). The recipes given here will improve your hair health!

Potato Juice

(To reduce hair fall)

Serves: 1

Ingredients:

- 2 medium potatoes, peeled

Directions:

1. Chop potatoes into chunks. Wash well.
2. Add potatoes into a blender along with some water.
3. Blend until smooth. Strain the juice.
4. Serve immediately, in between your meals. Do not have more than 1 glass in a day.

Fresh Orange Juice

(To reduce hair fall)

Serves: 1

Ingredients:

- 5–6 fresh oranges

Directions:

1. Wash the oranges and cut into 2 halves crosswise.
2. Juice the oranges with a citrus juicer.
3. Add some sweetener to taste if desired.
4. Serve with ice. Do not drink the juice on an empty stomach or before going to bed.

Amla Juice

(To increase hair growth)

Serves: 1

Ingredients:

- 1 ½ cups chopped Indian gooseberry (Amla)
- ¼ cup water
- Honey to taste (optional)

Directions:

1. Wash the gooseberries. Discard the pit and chop into pieces. Add amla and water into a blender and blend until smooth.
2. Strain the juice. You should get about ½ - ¾ cup of juice. Do not have more than ¾ cup in a day. Dilute with water if desired. After diluting, do not have more than a cup.
3. Add honey to taste if desired and drink it immediately after your meal. Do not have it on an empty stomach. Have it once a day.

Carrot Juice

(For hair growth)

Serves: 1

Ingredients:

- 8–10 carrots

Directions:

1. Wash the carrots.
2. Chop carrots into chunks.
3. Add carrots into a juicer and extract the juice. This juice can be had any time of the day or in between your meals. You can have up to 2 glasses of carrot juice in a day.

Aloe Vera Juice

(For hair growth and reduce dandruff)

Serves: 1

Ingredients:

- ½ cup fresh aloe Vera gel
- 1 teaspoon fresh lemon juice
- ½ cup water
- Honey to taste

Directions:

1. Take a piece from a fresh aloe Vera leaf. Slice off the thick green skin and measure out the pulp.
2. Add the pulp into a blender along with water. Blend until smooth.
3. Stir in honey and lemon juice.
4. Serve. This juice is most effective when you consume it on an empty stomach in the morning.
5. You can have up to 2 glasses of this juice in a day.

Spinach Juice

(To reduce hair fall)

Serves: 1

Ingredients:

- 2 cups fresh spinach leaves
- 2 inches fresh ginger
- Juice of ½ a lemon
- Honey to taste (optional)

Directions:

1. Wash the spinach and chop into large pieces.
2. Add spinach, lemon juice, ginger and a little water into a blender.
3. Blend until very well pureed. Strain the juice through a fine wire mesh strainer.
4. Add honey to taste and stir.
5. Serve.

Chapter 20:

Juices for Healthy Liver

The liver is one of the most important organs in the body. Did you know that it carries out over 500 roles in the body? It is the largest solid organ and the only one capable of regeneration. It helps produce bile, supports clotting of the blood, metabolizes fats and carbs, and stores vitamins and minerals. If the liver is not healthy or isn't functioning as intended, it results in a buildup of toxins (Arjun Kalra et al., 2022). It also harms the functioning of the digestive system and causes blood sugar fluctuations. Drinking wholesome fruit and vegetable juices given here helps improve liver health.

Liver Detoxifier

Serves: 2

Ingredients:

- 1 beet
- 4 carrots
- 1 bunch spinach

- Juice of a lemon
- 1 small bunch parsley
- 1 cucumber
- 6 celery sticks

Directions:

1. Wash all the vegetables.
2. Chop the beet and carrots into chunks.
3. Chop cucumber and celery into pieces. Tear the spinach and parsley.
4. Juice together beets, carrots, spinach, parsley, cucumber, and celery in a juicer.
5. Pour the juice into glasses and serve.

The Liver Scrubber Juice

Serves: 2

Ingredients:

- 8 medium carrots
- 2 whole beets
- 2 large apples, cored
- 6 beet green leaves
- 2 stalks celery
- 1 inch ginger

Directions:

1. Chop the apples, carrots, celery, beet greens (no stems) and beets cut into chunks.
2. Juice them all together in a juicer.
3. Pour into glasses and serve with crushed ice.

Herbs and Asparagus Juice

Serves: 1

Ingredients:

- ½ cucumber
- 5 sticks celery
- ½ cup chopped cilantro
- ½ cup chopped parsley
- 1 ounce Aloe Vera juice
- 2–3 asparagus spears
- 1 lemon

Directions:

1. Wash all the vegetables.
2. Peel lemon, Cut celery, asparagus, and cucumber into chunks.

3. Juice together cucumber, celery, cilantro, parsley, lemon, and asparagus in the juicer. Add aloe Vera juice and stir.
4. Pour into a glass. Add ice and serve.

Chapter 21:

Thirty Days of Juicing

Juicing is not only easy and convenient but is an incredible way to obtain all the needed nutrients. What more? You can whip up delicious and nutritious juices within a couple of minutes. Even drinking one healthy juice per day bridges any nutritional gaps in your daily requirements. In this section, you will be introduced to a variety of juices you can drink daily for 30 days to improve your overall health and achieve your weight loss and fitness goals.

(All the juices are for 1 serving)

Day 1: Ginger and lemon Juice

Ingredients:
- 1 head romaine hearts, chopped
- 1 cup chopped spinach
- 4 celery stalks, cut into 2 inch pieces
- Juice of 1/3 lemon
- ½ bunch of kale or collard greens
- 2 handfuls of parsley

- 1 (2-inches) piece of ginger

Directions:
1. Juice together all the vegetables in a juicer. Pour into a glass. Stir in lemon juice and serve.

Day 2: Mint and Berries Juice

Ingredients:
- 1 peeled kiwi fruit, chopped
- 1 cup of blueberries
- 1 cup mint leaves
- A handful strawberries, hulled, chopped

Directions:
1. Blend together the fruits and mint leaves in a blender until smooth.
2. Strain the juice and serve.

Day 3: Sweet Pineapple Juice

Ingredients:
- 1 cup cubed pineapple

- 3 cups chopped spinach
- 6 celery stalks, chopped into 2 inch pieces
- 12 kale leaves, chopped
- 1 small cucumber, peeled, chopped
- 1 (½ -inch) piece of ginger

Directions:

1. Juice together pineapple and vegetables in a juicer and serve.

Day 4: Spritzy Pomegranate-Blueberry Juice

Ingredients:

- 1 cups blueberries
- 1 ¼ cups pomegranate seeds

Directions:

1. Place pomegranate seeds and blueberries in a juicer and extract the juice.

Day 5: Savory Carrot Juice

Ingredients:

- 8 peeled carrots, chopped into chunks
- 2 cups trimmed wheatgrass

Directions:

1. Place some carrots in the juicer followed by wheatgrass.
2. Place remaining carrots in the juicer and extract the juice.

Day 6: Lavender and Pineapple Juice

Ingredients:

- 2 tbsp. fresh lavender blossoms
- 1 ½ cups peeled, cubed pineapple
- Lavender sprigs for garnish

Directions:

1. Blend together lavender blossoms and pineapple in a blender until smooth.
2. Strain the juice. Garnish with lavender sprigs and serve.

Day 7: Cucumber and Apple Juice

Ingredients:

- 7 kale leaves, chopped
- 1 small cucumber, chopped
- 1 apple, cored, chopped
- Juice of 1/3 lemon
- 1 cup chopped spinach
- 2 celery stalks, cut into 2 inch pieces
- 1 (½ inch) piece of ginger

Directions:

1. Juice together the apple and vegetables in a juicer.
2. Pour into a glass. Stir in lemon juice and serve.

Day 8: Bundling Carrots, Apples and Beets Juice

Ingredients:

- ½ pear, peeled, cored, chopped
- 1 ½ apples, peeled, cored
- 2 carrots, peeled, cubed

- 2 beets, peeled, cubed
- 1 cup of diced cabbage
- 6 handfuls chard

Directions:

1. Juice together the fruits and vegetables in a juicer.

Day 9: Smooth Juice of Apple Beet and Carrot

Ingredients:

- 2 diced apples
- 1 large carrots, skinned and sliced
- 2 handfuls spinach or kale
- 1 peeled and chopped beets
- 2 (1-inch) pieces of ginger

Directions:

1. Juice together the apples and vegetables in a juicer.

Day 10: Tropical Paradise

Ingredients:

- 1 cup peeled, cubed pineapple
- ½ pear, peeled, cored, cubed
- ½ cup blackberries
- 20 mint leaves
- 1 kiwifruit, peeled and diced

Directions:

1. Blend together the fruits and mint leaves in a blender until smooth.
2. Strain the juice and serve.

Day 11: Apples, Cantaloupe, and Honeydew Juice

Ingredients:

- 1 apple, cored, cubed
- ¼ honeydew melon, peeled, deseeded, cubed
- ¼ cantaloupe, peeled, deseeded, cubed
- 10 to 12 Swiss chard leaves, chopped
- 10 to 12 kale leaves, chopped

Directions:

1. Place fruits and greens in the juicer and extract the juice.

Day 12: Cucumber and Apple Juice

Ingredients:

- 5 kale leaves, chopped
- 1/3 cucumber, peeled, chopped
- 1 apple, peeled, cored, chopped
- 3 cups spinach
- 3 celery stalks, chopped into 2 inch pieces
- 1 (1/2inch) piece of ginger

Directions:

1. Juice together the vegetables and apple in a juicer.

Day 13: Sleek Beet Celeriac Carrot Juice

Ingredients

- 2–3 carrots, chopped
- 1 celeriac root, peeled, cubed
- 1 ½ apples, peeled, cored, chopped
- 2 beets, peeled, cubed
- 1 (½ inch) piece of ginger

Directions:

1. Juice together the vegetables and apple in a juicer.

Day 14: Carrot and Tomato Juice

Ingredients:

- 4 red beets, peeled, cubed
- 3 carrots, peeled, cubed
- 3 celery stalks, chopped into 2 inch pieces
- 5 plum tomatoes
- 5 cups roughly chopped packed parsley leaves and stems

- ½ jalapeño pepper, ribs and seeds removed
- 6 red radishes, cubed

Directions:

1. Juice together all the vegetables in a juicer and serve the juice.

Day 15: Carrots, Pineapples and Oranges Juice

Ingredients:

- 1 cup pineapple cubes
- 2 carrots, peeled, cubed
- 1 orange, peeled, seeded
- ½ lemon juice

Directions:

1. Juice together pineapple, carrots, and orange in a juicer.
2. Pour into a glass. Stir in lemon juice and serve

Day 16: Citrus cascade Juice

Ingredients:

- 4 cups of romaine hearts
- 2 oranges, peeled, separated into segments
- 4 celery stalks, chopped into pieces
- 1 Golden apple, cored, cubed
- 1 cucumber, cubed

Directions:

1. Place celery in the juicer followed by romaine hearts, apple, orange, and cucumber.
2. Extract the juice and serve.

Day 17: Beets and Oranges

Ingredients:

- 2 red beets, peeled, cubed
- 3 oranges, peeled, deseeded

Directions:

1. Place oranges and beets in the juicer and extract the juice.

Day 18: Pear and Fennel Juice

Ingredients

- 1 ½ medium fennel bulbs, peeled, cubed
- 1 Comice pear, cored, cubed

Directions:

1. Juice together pears and fennel in a juicer and serve.

Day 19: Tomatoes and Cucumber Juice

Ingredients:

- 2 plum tomatoes, halved or quartered
- 3 celery stalks, cut into 2 inch pieces
- 1/3 small red onion, cut into wedges
- Juice of ½ lime
- ½ large cucumber, peeled, chopped
- ½ red bell pepper, chopped
- 1 cup packed parsley leaves and stems, roughly chopped

Directions:

1. Blend together all the vegetables in a blender until smooth.
2. Strain the juice. Stir in lime juice and serve.

Day 20: Ginger and Blackberries Juice

Ingredients:

- 1 cup Concord grapes
- 4 (1-inch) pieces of ginger
- 2 Golden Delicious apples, peeled, cored, cubed
- 1 cup blackberries

Directions:

1. Blend together grapes, apples, ginger and blackberries in a blender until smooth.
2. Strain the juice and serve.

Day 21: Apples and Carrot Juice

Ingredients:

- 2 wedges red cabbage
- 1 ½ apples, peeled, cored, cubed

- 3 carrots, peeled, chopped
- 7–8 Swiss chard leaves, chopped
- 1 (2-inches) piece of ginger
- Juice of 1/3 lemon

Directions:
1. Juice together the vegetables in a juicer. Pour into a glass.
2. Stir in lemon juice and serve.

Day 22: The Green Delicacy Juice

Ingredients:
- 4 cups of beet greens, chopped or red Swiss chard or kale or spinach
- 1 pear, cored, cubed
- ½ apple, cored, cubed
- 6–7 strawberries
- ½ cup coconut water

Directions:
1. Place apple, greens, strawberries, and pear in the juicer and extract the juice.
2. Add coconut water and stir.
3. Serve.

Day 23: Spinach and Lemon Juice

- 2 green apples, peeled, cored, chopped
- 7 kale leaves, chopped
- 3 celery stalks, cut into 2 inch pieces
- 4 handfuls spinach
- ⅓ cucumber, peeled, chopped
- Juice of ⅔ lemon

Directions:
1. Juice together apples and vegetables in a juicer.
2. Pour the juice into a glass. Stir in lemon juice and serve.

Day 24: Yellowish Gold Juice

Ingredients:
- 2 sweet potatoes, peeled, sliced
- 2 cubed red bell peppers
- 1 ½ apples, cored, cubed
- 2 peeled and chopped carrots
- 4 beets, peeled, chopped
- 2 peeled and sliced oranges

Directions:

1. Juice together the vegetables and fruits in a juicer and serve.

Day 25: Celery and Spinach Juice

Ingredients:

- 2 fennel bulbs, cubed
- 2 celery stalks, cut into 2 inch pieces
- ½ large cucumber, peeled, cubed
- 1 ½ cups chopped spinach

Directions:

1. Juice together fennel, spinach, cucumber, and celery in a juicer.

Day 26: Oranges and Cranberry Juice

Ingredients:

- 1 cup cranberries
- 1 small Ruby Red grapefruit, peeled, separated into segments
- 3 limes, peeled, halved

- 3 (thumb-size) pieces of ginger
- 2 oranges, peeled, separated into segments

Directions:

1. Juice together ginger, limes, and fruits in a juicer.

Day 27: Kale and Ginger Juice

Ingredients

- 2 green apples, cored, cubed
- 3 large carrots
- 10 kale leaves
- 6 handfuls spinach
- 2 inches piece of ginger

Directions:

1. Juice together the apples and vegetables in a juicer.

Day 28: Lime and Apple Juice

Ingredients:

- ½ large cucumber, peeled, chopped
- 2 limes, peeled, halved
- 2 Golden Delicious apples
- 4 cups packed cilantro leaves and stems, roughly chopped
- 2 poblano pepper, ribs and seeds removed

Directions:

1. Juice together vegetables and apples in a juicer.

Day 29: Sour and Smooth Lemon Juice

Ingredients:

- 2 limes, peeled, quartered
- 2 lemons, peeled, quartered
- 1 green apple, cored, peeled, cubed
- 1 Asian pear, peeled, cored, cubed
- 4 carrots, peeled, cubed
- 4 cups shredded purple cabbage

- 2 (thumb-size) pieces of ginger

Directions:

1. Juice together the fruits and vegetables in a juicer and serve.

Day 30: Minty Strawberries and Pineapple Juice

Ingredients:

- 1 cup peeled, cubed pineapple
- ½ pear, peeled, cored, cubed
- ½ cup strawberries
- 20 mint leaves

Directions:

1. Juice together the fruit and mint leaves in a juicer and serve.

Conclusion

Now that you have come to the end of the book, you will have a clear idea about the different recipes that you like. Every recipe in the book has a clear set of instructions making it easier for you to prepare the juice. The ingredients in the recipe can improve your health in many ways. Each chapter is dedicated to different recipes you can use to improve your overall health.

It is important to remember that the ingredients in the recipe are not set in stone. You can tweak the recipes a little to suit your needs based on your understanding of nutrition and fresh ingredients.

I hope you and your family enjoy the recipes in the book, and your health improves.

References

Arakelyan, H. (n.d.). *(PDF) Hair and Food.* ResearchGate. Https://www.researchgate.net/publication/328802583_Hair_and_Food

Are There Health Benefits to Juicing? (2020, October 28). WebMD. https://www.webmd.com/diet/juicing-health-benefits

Cassidy, A., O'Reilly, É. J., Kay, C., Sampson, L., Franz, M., Forman, J. P., Curhan, G., & Rimm, E. B. (2011). Habitual intake of flavonoid subclasses and incident hypertension in adults. *The American Journal of Clinical Nutrition, 93*(2), 338–347. https://doi.org/10.3945/ajcn.110.006783

Donaldson, M. S. (2004). Nutrition and cancer: A review of the evidence for an anti-cancer diet. *Nutrition Journal, 3*(1). https://doi.org/10.1186/1475-2891-3-19

Esfahani, A., Wong, J. M. W., Truan, J., Villa, C. R., Mirrahimi, A., Srichaikul, K., & Kendall, C. W.

C. (2011). Health effects of mixed fruit and vegetable concentrates: a systematic review of the clinical interventions. *Journal of the American College of Nutrition*, *30*(5), 285–294. https://doi.org/10.1080/07315724.2011.10719971

Ghose, B., & Yaya, S. (2018). Fruit and vegetable consumption and anemia among adult non-pregnant women: Ghana Demographic and Health Survey. *PeerJ*, *6*. https://doi.org/10.7717/peerj.4414

Kalra, A., & Tuma, F. (2018, December 18). *Physiology, Liver*. Nih.gov; StatPearls Publishing. https://www.ncbi.nlm.nih.gov/books/NBK535438/

Kiefer, I., Prock, P., Lawrence, C., Wise, J., Bieger, W., Bayer, P., Rathmanner, T., Kunze, M., & Rieder, A. (2004). Supplementation with Mixed Fruit and Vegetable Juice Concentrates Increased Serum Antioxidants and Folate in Healthy Adults. *Journal of the American College of Nutrition*, *23*(3), 205–211. https://doi.org/10.1080/07315724.2004.10719362

Klinder, A., Shen, Q., Heppel, S., Lovegrove, J. A., Rowland, I., & Tuohy, K. M. (2016). Impact of increasing fruit and vegetables and flavonoid intake on the human gut microbiota. *Food & Function*, 7(4), 1788–1796. https://doi.org/10.1039/c5fo01096a

Lobo, V., Patil, A., Phatak, A., & Chandra, N. (2010). Free radicals, Antioxidants and Functional foods: Impact on Human Health. *Pharmacognosy Reviews*, 4(8), 118–126. https://doi.org/10.4103/0973-7847.70902

Murphy, M., Stettler, N., Reiss, R., & Smith, K. (2014). Associations of consumption of fruits and vegetables during pregnancy with infant birth weight or small for gestational age births: a systematic review of the literature. *International Journal of Women's Health*, 899. https://doi.org/10.2147/ijwh.s67130

Ravn-Haren, G., Dragsted, L. O., Buch-Andersen, T., Jensen, E. N., Jensen, R. I., Németh-Balogh, M., Paulovicsová, B., Bergström, A., Wilcks, A., Licht, T. R., Markowski, J., & Bügel, S. (2012). Intake of whole apples or clear apple juice has contrasting effects on plasma lipids in healthy volunteers. *European Journal of Nutrition*, 52(8),

1875–1889. https://doi.org/10.1007/s00394-012-0489-z

Wang, P.-Y., Fang, J.-C., Gao, Z.-H., Zhang, C., & Xie, S.-Y. (2015). Higher intake of fruits, vegetables or their fiber reduces the risk of type 2 diabetes: A meta-analysis. *Journal of Diabetes Investigation*, *7*(1), 56–69. https://doi.org/10.1111/jdi.12376

Zhang, Y.-J., Gan, R.-Y., Li, S., Zhou, Y., Li, A.-N., Xu, D.-P., & Li, H.-B. (2015). Antioxidant Phytochemicals for the Prevention and Treatment of Chronic Diseases. *Molecules*, *20*(12), 21138–21156. https://doi.org/10.3390/molecules201219753

Printed in Great Britain
by Amazon